Sowing in Tears II

Sowing in Tears II

When Brokenness Becomes Beauty

LEEANN HALE

Email—sowingintearsbook@gmail.com
Facebook—https://www.facebook.com/sowingintearsbook
Instagram—@sowingintearsbook

©Leeann Hale 2022

Print ISBN: 978-1-66786-957-5
eBook ISBN: 978-1-66786-958-2

*Please note: all scripture quotations are taken from the English Standard Version (Crossway, 2001) unless otherwise noted.

Contents

Adoption symbol: Each point of the triangle represents the birth-parents, adoptive parents and the adoptee. The heart surrounding the triangle represents the love that unites them.

Acknowledgements

Write *a book*, they said. *You have to finish your story*, they said.

And I said, "Um, maybe you haven't noticed, but I have four boys five and under. My time is not my own, and speaking of time, I have none."

With every person who asked, each one chipped away at my secret urge of writing a sequel and finishing our story. So much has changed since writing my first book. Our family looks completely different and even some of my mindset has changed in the way I view life through the eyes of adoption.

I'd like to give a heartfelt thank you to everyone who kept politely pestering me. I am thrilled to share the rest of our story after publishing *Sowing in Tears: A Mother's Sorrow in Infertility and Joy in Adoption.*

I'd also like to thank my faithful husband who believes and encourages me through all my endeavors, especially thinking I could tackle another book while raising four on-the-go little boys. He is a huge reason why this book is in your hands now and not still a word document on my computer. Without his support, I couldn't have done this.

Publishing a book forces you to become vulnerable. But entrusting someone with the first draft of your book and welcoming critiques places a whole new meaning on the word. My editor, J. Carl White, took my book to another level. He (politely) forced me to push through and reminisce on some painful moments of my story to give the scenes the rhetorical appeal they deserved. He encouraged and guided me in the editing process from start to finish, and to say *I'm thankful* would be an understatement.

I can't think of anyone better to write the forward to my book other than Grace. She truly lives a life fitting to her name. I'm beyond thankful to God for placing her in my life. She would tell you that I have been a mentor to her, but the truth is, though she may be younger in years, she has encouraged my heart on countless occasions. She radiates grace and beauty in all she does and her testimony of living a surrendered life to Christ is truly remarkable.

Thank you to my favorite blessings: Jayden, Jaxon, Jordan and Joshua. Your lives are my greatest treasure!

Dedication

My favorite guys!

My husband who demonstrates the hands and feet of Jesus to his whole family and my boys who demonstrate endless patience and grace to their mother who is constantly learning and navigating motherhood!

You five are my heart! I love you endlessly!

Foreword

I have had the pleasure of knowing Leeann and her family for several years through the wonderful church we both attend and then, knowing her more personally as she and Zach serve as the leaders of our college group. Zach and Leeann are wonderful teachers, encouragers, and parents. Their boys are energetic, spunky, and fun to be around (and, a bit of trivia, I share the same birthday as Jayden and Joshua—a fun bonus!). Getting to see their family grow over the years has been such a joy and a touching reminder of the LORD's steadfast love. In the time I have known Leeann, it has been made abundantly clear again and again how much she loves her boys, how changed her life has been because of them, and how—even through her inadequacies—God has remained faithful and carried out His perfect plan through her life.

Adoption is something very close to my heart because it is an integral part of my personal story. I was adopted at 10 months old from Ma'anshan, China into a Caucasian American family who instantly took me in as their own. I have five siblings, and though none of them are genetically related to me, or slightly resemble me in any way, they are just as much a part of me as if we were flesh and blood.

Growing up, my parents made sure to always let me know that I was just as much their daughter as the biological children were. They never hid the fact that I had joined the family in a different-but-equally-special way (although, truthfully, it would be hard for anyone to believe that two white parents gave birth to an Asian daughter...) and, rather, celebrated it. Adoption is beautiful because it reminds us of how God, in His abundant mercy and grace (my namesake!), saw us in our brokenness and took us in. We were alone and helpless, and He sent His only Son to die in our place so that we could be His children.

"See what kind of love the Father has given to us, that we should be called children of God; and so we are." (1 John 3:1)

We who were once lost and in need of a father can now enter into a personal relationship with our Heavenly Father and Creator. We who were once in the wilderness can now partake in joy and life eternal. And, what's more, before we even thought to seek or acknowledge Him, He was loving and pursuing us. He chose us as His own. This is the truth my parents pointed me back to and ingrained in me. This is the love that I have known.

That's not to say that it has not been very hard at times. Like everything else, adoption has its ups and downs. I'd like to dispel the notion that an adoptee's unrest regarding their past stems from a lack of something in their adoptive family. My parents made sure I lacked nothing and loved me even before I was officially a Daniels. My siblings have never treated me any differently and are some of my closest friends. Yet, still, the pain remains.

There have been many tears shed over unanswered questions, many aching moments of frustration and anger at the brokenness of the world. There have been days that I looked in the mirror with distaste at my almond-shaped eyes, dark hair, and Eastern Asian features—partly because I didn't look like anyone I knew (growing up mainly in the south and overseas in Europe meant getting to see very little of other Asians), and partly because I didn't know the faces that had led to the formation of my own. To those of you who know your biological family, I beg that you never take it for granted. I would give anything to sit around with my biological parents and trace their faces with my fingers to see exactly whose nose, whose eyes, whose smile, I got. I have wept over the fact that I may never be out doing a menial task with my birth mother, only to be stopped by the words: "You are *definitely* your mother's girl. I can see the resemblance." Or that I may never get to sit around listening to the story of how my parents met, what they were like as kids, and whose personality more closely resembles mine.

Although my life has been full of joy and I wouldn't change it at all, I cannot help but mourn the loss of the life I could have had. The life which the evil of the world forced my birth parents to give me up, thus shattering our family into separate pieces strewn across the globe. I cannot help but grieve over the hurt and the difficulty of the decision my birth parents had to make, and that same decision that countless mothers and families are having to make every day. To give up one's baby for the sake of that child's life being made better is one of the most selfless, yet painful loves. I am honored to be a walking testimony of that love.

In a perfect world, there would be no broken families and, thus, no need for adoption. However, while we are on this side of eternity, we inhabit a fallen world, which means grappling with the consequences of sin. As believers, we are called to tend to the hurting, the widows, and the orphans. And how can we not, when we have been privy to such a love as that which we have been shown?

Adoption doesn't just mean the joys of having a new child added to *your* home. It also means that, somewhere on this earth, there is another home with one less child—and that is no small thing. It means teaching your child about where they came from and how it reflects God's love for us. It means sitting with them and just praying or being present when the questions with no answers come. It means gaining a deeper understanding of how tenderly the Father chose us.

It is joyful and tearful and messy, but it is so rewarding for all parties involved. A family being patched together not by DNA, but by love. That is the heart of Christ.

Grace Daniels / 马幸莉 (Ma Xing Li)

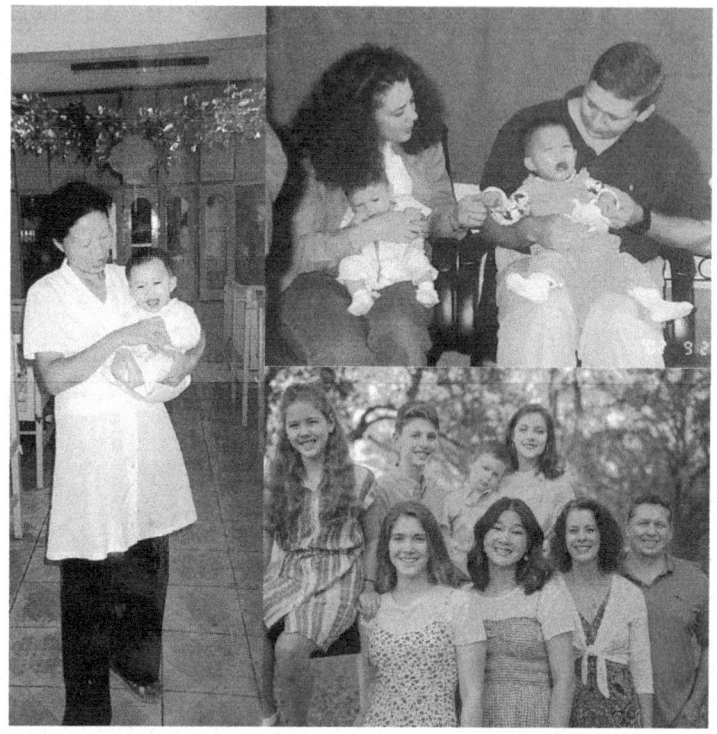

[Me with my caretaker in the orphanage, circa 2002; Meeting my parents and new sister, Rachel, for the first time, September 22, 2002; Family photo, March 2020]

Child Survey

Jayden—Age 5, Jaxon—Age 3

1. What is something mommy always says to you?

    Jayden — "Time to eat. It's 'cause we eat all the time."

    Jaxon — "I love you."

2. How does mommy make you laugh?

    Jayden — "Sticking Joshua's booty butt in my face."

    Jaxon — *puts fingers in mouth to spread his mouth open and sticks his tongue out*

3. What's your favorite thing about daddy?

    Jayden — "When he tickles me and plays with me outside."

    Jaxon — "When he plays frisbee with me. When he tickles me."

4. What's your favorite thing about mommy?

    Jayden — "When we lay on your bed reading books."

    Jaxon — "When you sit with me."

5. How old is mommy?

    Jayden — "31, no 32."

    Jaxon — "I don't remember it."

6. How tall is mommy?

    Jayden — "100."

    Jaxon — "Like that tall." *points to the top of my head*

7. What is mommy really good at?

Jayden — "Singing and taking care of babies."

Jaxon — "Working."

8. What is something mommy isn't very good at?

Jayden — "I don't know. That's a hard one."

Jaxon — "I don't know."

9. What is mommy's job?

Jayden — "Clean the dishwasher."

Jaxon — "Laundry."

10. What is your favorite day of the week?

Jayden — "Saturday because daddy doesn't have to work and he makes eggs and bacon."

Jaxon — "I like playing Mario."

11. Favorite part about your adoption story?

Jayden — "When I got to sit with you in the hospital. And I got to look at you. That's my favorite thing I like to do. And my favorite part of adoption is that I love my birth mom and dad."

Jaxon — "When I was a baby, because I like that part."

12. Who is God?

Jayden — "Our Heavenly Father. Holy. Jehovah Jireh."

Jaxon — "In Heaven."

13. What has God done in your life?

> Jayden — "He created me. He gave me my birth mom and dad. He fixes the stuff that's hard for us."

> Jaxon — "Helped me with my attitude."

14. What are you thankful for?

> Jayden — "That God gave me a house to live in. That he gave us Jesus to die on the cross."

> Jaxon — "I'm thankful he changed my life. That he gave us a mommy and daddy."

15. What does it mean to be a christian?

> Jayden — "Repent. Believe in God. To know God. Believe that Jesus died on the cross for our sins."

PS. Don't read mommy's book until you read the first one. I'm the oldest. It's only fair you hear my story before you hear about my little brothers.

—Jayden

Part One:
Looking Back

For my thoughts are not your thoughts, neither are your ways my ways, declares the Lord. For as the heavens are higher than the earth, so are my ways higher than your ways and my thoughts than your thoughts.

(Isaiah 55:8-9)

1
Reaching From Empty

⬦

T oday marked my 32nd year around the sun. 11,680 days of existence on planet earth. Joshua was sucking down bottle number—I lost track—for the day and I sat, sobbing, staring at the blank wall in front of me in my bedroom. I clutched a pillow close against my chest and curled under my covers. The three other boys were tucked into bed and the special dinner Zach bought for my birthday was finally warming in the oven because a last minute basketball practice got added to the schedule and we all missed dinner.

Is this how my life would continue for the remainder of the parenting years ahead?

If so, I didn't know if I could take another moment. My life was nothing like I pictured it would have been five years prior. Life was more than I had ever hoped or prayed for and a nightmare all wrapped up in one. Four babies barely five and under and the youngest two only 15 months apart. Our days seemed to constantly resemble a state of chaos while I yearned for tidiness and order. And after the days were through, I could only seem to remember the arguing and disobedience, yet I fought so hard to remember the good. Exhaustion replaced rest, and it seemed the slightest thing could tip me over my breaking point. I felt inadequate and ill equipped to be the mother my children deserved. Mornings would start out precious and sweet but by the time Zach was home from work, he too often witnessed the worst version of his wife and mother to his children. By the evenings, it seemed as though the energy that carried me through the day had vanished.

I envisioned *that mom*. The one who planned crafts and activities corresponding to the season, park adventures, and baking lessons in the kitchen. I imagined *that mom* who cut up the fruit for her kids' lunches to resemble fun shapes. *That mom* who wrote accompanying napkin notes, and led crafts at the dining room table that left everyone messy from head to toe but smiling and laughing the whole way through.

My kids would love that mom.

She sounded so fun and so full of energy with joy bursting from her seams. I bet *that mom* also has a big pot roast in the oven with a cute little apron waiting patiently at the door to greet her husband after a long day of work.

My husband would love that wife.

I wanted to be that mom for my kids. I wanted to be that wife for my husband. I desperately wanted to give each one all of me and more, but I felt as though I was reaching into an empty cistern.

How could I give from empty?

What I wish I knew in that moment is a lesson I learned several months later, a lesson of contentment. I learned to rest in the knowledge that the mother I am will *never* be enough for my family. The wife I am will *never* be enough for my husband. But, thankfully my family doesn't *just* get me. They get a package deal. I will never be enough for my family alone, but my Lord Almighty, my El Shaddai, *He* is more than enough. He is sufficient for all that we ask or think, according to the power at work within us (Ephesians 3:20). Christ's strength is magnified in my weakness (2 Corinthians 12:9) and His cistern never runs dry. When even my husband doesn't understand the depths of despair I feel at times in my inadequacies, I am loved by the One who clothes the lilies in grandeur and watches over every sparrow that fills the skies. If he cares for the flowers of the field and the birds of the sky, how much more does He care for me, His child (Matthew 6:26)?

After letting me explode on him, I fell into the arms of my patient husband. "Can you please just pray for me?" I begged in desperation. "I've prayed so much and I need someone else to pray because God's not hearing my prayers anymore." As I uttered the words, I knew it wasn't true, but in the moment I felt the most honest I had been in a long while. The past year had been one of the most joy-filled and one of the hardest years of my life. And as I was about to embark on year 32, it looked as if the hard would outweigh the joy.

Lord don't let that be so!

To paint a picture of how I arrived *here* I need to rewind[1] the tape about four years.

---

1. If you haven't already read *Sowing in Tears: A Mother's Sorrow in Infertility and Joy in Adoption*, you should do so before continuing or you'll be missing out on a whole lot more.

2

God is Gracious

Jayden was perfect—as close to perfect as one can be without truly holding the unattainable gift of perfection. If I could have dreamed up a child on my own accord, I never would have come close to anyone as wonderful as our boy. His whole being manifested joy. As a baby, Jayden left the hospital on a great schedule, and that continued at home! He ate well, slept well, and giggled constantly. Everything suddenly became more fun with him: evening walks around the neighborhood, holidays, parties, trips. Everything!

In the spring of 2018, when Jayden was about a year and a half, we decided we wanted to grow our family once again. If God saw fit to bless us with another child, we wanted them to be close in age so they could grow up having a built-in best friend. We looked into both foster care and adoption attorneys and God made it clear, through a series of events, that working with an adoption attorney was the direction He was leading us at that specific time. In January of 2018, we contacted the same adoption attorney who had finalized Jayden's adoption back in 2017. Working with her for a second time somehow brought added comfort. Much like with Jayden's adoption, we hit the ground running. Except this time, we were seasoned veterans. Familiarity hovered over the routine, the paperwork, and the appointments. We completed our paperwork just as quickly as the first time around—if not more quickly.

Our church was having its annual kid's camp—our version of vacation bible school—and I wore the "lead crafter" hat. At the time, my husband and I had been members of our church for roughly five years. Shortly after we became members, we began helping with the youth group. And shortly after posting a picture to Facebook of the latest craft I had created, I found out that our Pastor was serious when he talked about members of the body using their gifts. He saw my Facebook post and called to ask if I would lead crafts for camp.

One of the elders at our church owns several acres of land where he and his wife built *Peaceful Way*. This was a place where people could gather for events, outreach ministries, or just to enjoy the quiet outdoors with family and friends. All the kids looked forward to summer camp here year after year. Cows, horses, even lemurs were known to graze the fields. A beautiful backyard swimming pool welcomed a myriad of children from multiple age groups, and children's songs and laughter spread throughout the grounds.

I'm a very detail oriented person, so being on time equates to being late in my book. I pulled up to Peaceful Way early enough that I had to enter the security gate code before the gate would open and allow my entrance. As I punched the numbers into the pinpad, my phone rang. Back in May, we were officially considered "active" for our adoption and any potential expectant mother could view our profile. Fast forward two months, to July 11th, and our adoption attorney was calling me after hours on a Wednesday evening. My fingers trembled as I pressed *answer* and cleared my throat.

Am I the only one who clears her throat prior to answering phone calls? I don't do it when someone comes up to me in passing, so why do I have the incessant need to clear my throat only upon answering important phone calls? And why was she calling me after hours? Couldn't whatever she needed wait until morning when she was in her office? Unless it couldn't. Unless maybe, just maybe this was the phone call? Surely it couldn't be.

When we heard the news about Jayden after only 15 days of being active, our agency was very quick to tell us and remind us on multiple occasions, "This never happens. This seriously never happens."

There's no way it could be possible that another adoption would come after only a few short weeks of waiting.

Let me remind you, this was the back and forth conversation I had with myself all before answering my phone. What a chatterbox my ever-running brain could be.

"Hey, Emily," I answered, confused but excited.

Here's my best recollection of the next few moments:

"Leeann, sorry to bother you right around dinner time. But I wanted to present a situation to you."

"Sure! I'm actually not with Zach right now. Do you want me to add him to the call?"

"Yeah, that would be great," she answered.

Frantically I began trying to dial him in and merge calls. I was a teenager through the evolution of cell phones. This should be a very simple task. Instead, I felt weighed down by a true heaviness of complexity. 50,000 minutes later I finally merged all three of us on a single call.

"Hey Emily. I'm on the line now," Zach chimed in.

"Hey there, Zach. I was just telling Leeann I had a situation I wanted to run by y'all. I just got off the phone with an expectant mother and she has chosen you both."

"Oh my word! Wow!" was somehow the only intelligent thing I could muster up.

"I'm still working on getting more information for you. She has a due date of August 1st, and just completed an ultrasound and everything seemed to look good from what I understand. Other than that, I don't have any prenatal information for you right now. She is no longer in a relationship with her boyfriend, but he does know about the adoption and he actually chose y'alls profile separately from her. Kind of a funny story, I'll tell ya about it later."

"Ok, wow. That's awesome." Again, lacking in any attempt at more mature adjectives to contribute to this conversation.

"I'll let y'all talk it over and if you could get back to me I will let her know your answer and we will move forward however you decide".

"Ok, that sounds great. Thank you so much. You definitely made our night. We'll get back to you very soon."

Triple checking to make sure Zach and I were the only ones left on the line, we had a moment of celebration. *What in the world? How on earth?* We knew we had lots to talk about, but we exchanged ecstatic *I love yous* and knew we'd talk when I got home.

Though I say we had lots to talk about, I think both of our minds were already made up almost instantaneously after we hung up with our adoption attorney. I got home from camp and we both were ready to move forward with this potential placement. The next few days escaped in a blur, but one thing seemed certain. Jayden was about to be a big brother. His one year old voice couldn't quite articulate "brother" yet, but he sure did try and "bubby" is what came out and, in my completely unbiased opinion, that's one hundred times cuter than "brother" anyway.

Sporadically throughout the day, Jayden and I would pray for "bubby." Driving to the grocery store or sitting on the living room couch, Jayden prayed: "Be with bubby. Amen." If only technology was advanced enough to insert a video into a paperback book. If I could, I would. The prayers were precious. And how much more precious would this new little bundle of joy be?

Four days later brought us to Sunday morning. Being parents to only one child meant we could lazily drag our feet on Sunday mornings and still be on time for church. Zach unplugged his phone and realized he had a missed text from the middle of the night. I checked my phone and I too had an email from the same time. Both were from our attorney. We called her back immediately, and much to our surprise, found out our expectant mother went into early labor in the middle of the night, and was due to deliver within the next few hours. We both frantically started running around the house putting together a diaper bag of items for bubby and restocking Jayden's diaper bag. We called one of our friends from church and explained the situation. No sooner did I try to ask for a huge favor than they immediately took the words out of my mouth. "Just drop Jayden off at church this morning on your way to the hospital. We'll bring him back to our place for lunch after the service. Take your time at the hospital. We have a pack n' play so Jayden can spend the night with us too. We'd love to have him. We're so excited and will be praying for y'all." What an amazing church body we have. People truly acted as the hands and feet of Jesus in our time of need. We took them up on their generous offer and rushed like mad people around our home.

Today is the day!

Zach and I constantly bumped into each other scurrying around the house to accomplish our to do list of tasks before walking out the door. The car ride to the hospital seemed to take forever. We cried, laughed, prayed, and nervously played through every scenario in our minds. Zach dropped me off at the hospital and then drove to drop Jayden off at church with our friends. I walked in, hesitant on how to feel in the moment. I truly had no idea what to expect from the situation. Was this a joyful moment? *Yes!* Was this a moment of deep confusion? *Yes!*

Is it ok to be excited? Is it ok to be happy when down the hall a woman's heart is breaking?

Our attorney instructed us beforehand to go to the nurses' station to let them know we had arrived and to explain our situation. So you better believe the nurses' station was my first stop. I was greeted by the sweetest nurse who already knew my name and stood ready to meet me. "Yes, she told us about you. You can feel free to go wait in our waiting room and we will keep you posted on her progress."

"Thank you so much. Please let her know we are here, and if she needs anything at all we're just a few doors down and are ready and wanting to help in any way possible," I replied.

I walked back to the waiting room, heart pounding and mind racing.

Is she all alone? Does anyone else know she's here?

We still hadn't seen a picture of her or the baby's father so with each man that walked in I wondered if it was him.

Is he walking back there to be with her? Did we just make eye contact unknowingly?

Another family shared the hospital waiting room. Their daughter-in-law had given birth overnight and they and the siblings were all taking turns going in and meeting the newest member of the family. I couldn't wait for our turn.

Did she already have the baby? Is she in active labor right now as I'm sitting in this chair? Is she holding her baby, looking into his eyes, and contemplating the biggest decision of her life?

No sooner had I wished Zach would hurry up and save me from my perpetual thoughts than I saw him walking down the hall into the waiting room. My life saver. Now would begin a full day of waiting.

Throughout the day we stayed in contact with our attorney. An unrelated pressing situation had her immediate attention, but she promised she would hurry to get to the hospital to meet with us as soon as she could. Several hours and many prayers passed by, and our attorney gave me instructions to go back to the nurses' station to relay a message for her. I was excited for an excuse to go back to speak with the nurse and hopefully get an update. As I walked down the hallway I spotted the same friendly nurse I had spoken to earlier that morning. I walked up to her only to be greeted in a cold presence. I don't even remember our exchange now, but what I do remember is feeling about two inches tall and like not a single person wanted me anywhere near there. I quickly apologized—not exactly knowing what I was apologizing for—and walked back to the waiting room to the one person in the hospital I knew would welcome me with open arms. Embarrassed, heartbroken, and confused I buried my head in Zach's chest and started crying.

"She was so rude to me. I don't even know what I did. I just told her what I was supposed to tell her. That's all. The nurse was totally different. When I went in this morning she was so sweet to me. Something is wrong. I don't know what it is, but something is wrong. It's just all so different now."

Seconds turned to minutes which turned to hours and the waiting became brutal. We were emotional in every sense of the word. Our attorney finally showed up sometime that evening and after a series of events told us to go home and come back tomorrow morning. Utterly exhausted, we gathered our things, headed to the car and drove straight to Jayden. I couldn't wait to see him. After the day we had, he would be my ray of sunshine. I walked through the doorway and his wobbly, unsteady legs came running up to me with a smile plastered on his face. Oh, how I loved my sweet boy. His hug was exactly what I needed.

Monday morning we woke up to the *same* bated breath, the *same* fear, and the *same* excitement. We dropped Jayden off with the *same* friends and arrived at the *same* hospital for another day of waiting. As we sat together in the hard, uncomfortable waiting room chairs we shared many prayers, both together and individually crying out to God.

I remember as vividly as the anticipation grew with each moment, a specific prayer I prayed on repeat to God. A prayer I never even shared with Zach until days later. Not purposefully, but a prayer I truly cried out to God in my deepest most sincere desperation. "God, Your will be done." I can't count the number of times I prayed those words in the hospital waiting room, or sang the words to the song "Thy Will" as I drove to and from the hospital.

> *I don't wanna think*
> *I may never understand*
> *That my broken heart is a part of Your plan*
> *When I try to pray*
> *All I've got is hurt and these four words*
> *Thy will be done*[2]

Throughout the three decades I've been alive, I admit to praying prayers I didn't mean in the moment. Either praying them out of habit, or feeling pressured by the situation, but praying for God's will to be done in this very situation was one of the hardest, most genuine prayers I think I have ever prayed to God. I desperately wanted to bring this child home as our son. My heart had his name written all over it. I loved him like I loved Jayden and I hadn't even seen him

---

2.   Bernie Herms, Hillary Scott, Emily Weisband. EMI Nashville. 2016.

yet. But at the same time, as a mother myself, I knew that wasn't my prayer to pray. I could love him endlessly as if he was my child—and I did, but I didn't have the right to pray for him to *be* my child.

It wasn't my prayer to pray.

Instead, I prayed on repeat: *God, Your will be done.*

Our attorney met us at the hospital Monday afternoon. The waiting room continued to fill with more families, so she brought us to a more secluded section of the hospital where we could talk. My heart sank in the short walk to the new set of chairs.

Why can't she just tell us whatever she has to say right here? Why do we have to go somewhere more private? What did she find out in the previous hours as we waited tirelessly pacing holes in the floors of the hospital?

"Thank you guys for your patience today. I know it's been pretty uncertain the last 24 plus hours."

I don't need a pacifier. Just spit it out.

"It's looking like there is a very good chance this could result in a failed match. Originally, the expectant mother hadn't told anyone about the pregnancy, but she has since called her own mother and her mother is assuring her that she will help raise the baby. Nothing is decided yet, but she would like some time to think about it and she has asked for you both to go home now rather than wait at the hospital. I can't tell you why these things happen sometimes. All I can say is that God has a reason and we may never know."

My heart sank deeper into my chest, my stomach ached, and my teeth only bit harder into my tongue in an attempt to stop the tears from pouring out of my eyes in front of a hospital full of strangers. Even after this news, the majority of my thinking told me this baby would still be coming home with us. Maybe not today, but soon. Not because I felt I deserved him more than his own mother, but because I truly felt for the past week, especially the past two days, that he was our son. There's no way, after all the emotional investment, that it wouldn't work out in that manner.

A week ago she was so confident in her decision of adoption. She was so confident in choosing our family. She was adamant that nothing would change her mind.

On the drive home I gave my tongue a break from the teeth bites and allowed the tears to flow.

I didn't know she wanted us gone. I never would have stayed if I knew that. I never wanted her to feel uncomfortable. I knew it was true, but for whatever reason I felt the need to defend myself.

I walked into an empty house to wait alone with Jayden while Zach went back to work. I envied that he had something to keep his mind busy. There was nothing for me to do. I prayed on repeat and checked my phone on the minute to make sure I hadn't missed a message from our attorney.

The day dragged on and still no news. Tuesday passed with the same deafening silence. Wednesday morning arrived and Zach headed off to work again leaving me and Jayden alone at home once more. I texted Zach mid morning: "I'm feeling a lot better about this. I haven't gotten an email from the attorney yet, so I'm taking that as good news. I don't think this is going to result in a failed match." He texted back a simple, "I love you," and was home shortly after.

As he walked through the door, I greeted him with hopeful anticipation. I knew he was probably overwhelmed and it was my turn to speak life and positivity into him.

"It's ok. I really am feeling a lot better about all this. I think no news is probably good news at this point," I said, smiling and welcoming him home with a hug.

"Can you come sit down on the couch with me?" He motioned me over, almost oblivious to the words I had just spoken.

"The attorney called me about an hour ago. The mother changed her mind. Our attorney said when there's a failed match she calls the husband first so they can share with their wives. That's why you haven't heard from her. I love you so much, you know that?"

If there was ever a time I wished I wasn't so wrong, it was here and now in this very moment. Once again, I fell in his arms and cried. And as I did, the tiny hand of our one year old came over to wipe a tear from my face. I picked him up into my arms and held him close as his daddy held me. We had all lost something today, but we lost something that was never ours to begin with. The emotion wrapped up in that package of confusion was impossible to understand. I posted this to facebook a few days later:

> We serve a GOOD God, even in the pain and uncertainty! On April 2nd, Zach and I experienced the excitement of our first pregnancy with the heartache of our first miscarriage almost simultaneously. But even in that time of pain, God was still GOOD and we knew His plans for our family were in His hands! Last Wednesday (July 11) our attorney presented us with an expectant mother who had chosen us to parent her child (with a due date of August 1). On Sunday, we got the call saying she was in labor. We rushed to find child care for Jayden and headed straight for the hospital. We stayed all day Sunday and part of the day Monday in the hospital with no answers. Today, we waited all day for news only to find out that the mother had changed her mind and her family had agreed to help her raise her baby. It's hard for people, not in our position, to understand the emotional toll this takes. Crying in Zach's arms tonight as he told me this news, God gave a simple reminder that He had not forsaken us through the tiny hand of our son coming up to wipe away my tears. We may never know why God allowed both these situations

to play out the way they did, but we can rest in knowing that He is STILL good! In the saddest times and in the happiest times. His ways are better than our ways and our prayer is that in this time, He would be glorified. Our constant prayer over the last few days was that HIS WILL be done, so we can only trust that this baby is in the loving arms of his family. We ask for continued prayer for this mother and her precious baby as they adjust to a new life. Thank you all who have reached out with prayers and support. We want to share our WHOLE story, even the messy parts, because God uses EVERY part to work His perfect will.

Failed match!

I hate that phrase! But at the time it was all I knew. What we went through, what this mother went through wasn't a *fail*. It was painful, beautiful, heart wrenching, and healing all in one, which is exactly what adoption is. Adoption is pain and beauty coinciding. It's sorrow and joy wrapped together in a bow of unconditional love. We didn't experience a *failed* match. We experienced *love*! We lived out a love for this baby that was so instant and so intimate we truly felt this child was our son from the moment we found out about him. Simultaneously, we witnessed a mother who didn't feel she had the support or resources to give her child what she felt he needed and then when she realized she *did*, and she *could* provide for him, she chose to in a heartbeat. A *failed match* is the opportunity to observe one of the purest demonstrations of love.

Weeks later, God gave us a glimpse into His sovereignty and how He intricately wove our stories together for our good and His glory. Oftentimes in life, when trials come and headaches occur, we have to settle with the unknowns of why a good and loving God would allow such pain. As a follower of Jesus, I have a hope unlike the world. I hold a hope that is steady and sure and provides a peace beyond any human understanding, reminding me that God is *for* me and His plans are far better than mine even in the times I don't understand. Many times in life I have had to settle for simply trusting God, knowing that I will never understand His reasoning on this side of Heaven. Trusting in His sovereignty is terrifying. I know He is good. I know He is faithful. I know He is my firm foundation. But seeing the "bigger picture" and why He allows certain plans to unfold would make trusting Him so much easier. However, it is clear from Scripture that our minds simply can't grasp the complexity of God's divine nature: "For my thoughts are not your thoughts, neither are your ways my ways, declares the Lord. For as the heavens are higher than the earth, so are my ways higher than your ways and my thoughts than your thoughts" (Isaiah 55:8-9).

As I previously mentioned, this mother never shared her pregnancy with any of her family or friends. When she went into labor for the first time in her life, no one knew. She had no one to call, no one to text, and no one to confide in. She experienced the most terrifying, beautiful, and amazing moment of her life completely alone. I can't begin to comprehend the strength she displayed in walking through nine months of pregnancy knowing in the end she would be alone and empty handed, but counting the life of her child as so precious that she willingly faced these immense fears. I was reminded that God was indeed working in the midst of our tangled story. If Zach and I had never been presented with even the possibility of adopting her son, she would have had no one praying on her behalf. But from the moment we were matched, we prayed fervently for her. We prayed fervently for her son. When we learned she went into early labor, during those days of complete unknowns, we prayed fervently for them both! Although circumstances seemed to say she was *alone*, she had two people just a few doors down the hall from her hospital room covering her and her son in prayer. Beauty was surrounding me though I felt broken.

I still ache reminiscing on the pain we felt when we learned she changed her mind on adoption. But I would go back again a thousand times to the sorrow and joy, excitement and fear, certainties and unknowns knowing exactly how the story would end. I never caught her eyes. I never held her hand. I never spoke a single word to her. But *God* saw her in her brokenness. *God* held her in the palm of His mighty, omnipotent hand. *God* spoke life into us both. God brought us together in a moment where she needed *Him* far more than she needed me. The simple prayer, "God, Your will be done" has brought comfort to me on many occasions. I can rest in knowing that her sweet little boy is exactly where he is supposed to be. From the outside looking in, it would seem as though my prayers brought me loss, when in reality, that single prayer brought restoration and unification. I can smile through the tears because my God remains faithful. I want my testimony to shout His praise just as loudly in the valleys as on the mountaintops. Through my years of infertility, my miscarriage, and then this unexpected news, my God was and is still seated on His throne, still in control, and I still choose to praise His name.

Exactly seven days later, I emailed our attorney regarding some specifics involving our situation. I was used to waiting sometimes a couple of days before receiving a response back, but much to my surprise I received a phone call later that same evening.

Why is she calling us now? I didn't ask anything too important. And certainly not important enough for her to call me after hours again.

Zach sat in the living room just a few feet away, and I answered the phone.

"Hello?"

"Hey Leeann, sorry to bother you right around supper time but I have some news that just came to my attention. I had an expectant mother contact me today and she has chosen you and Zach. She saw your adoption profile along with the video online and she has a baby boy due next month."

I frantically grabbed the junk mail envelope sitting on the counter and began scribbling down everything she said. Once again, she told me to talk it over with Zach and to get back to her when we had an answer.

I hung up and stood in shock.

Is this really happening all over again? And so soon after last week's events?

Once again, it didn't take much contemplating on our end. We gave our attorney the go ahead the next morning. This began a series of back and forth conversations between me and our expectant mother (to protect her privacy, I will refer to her as Sydney). Having open communication, especially prior to the birth, was very new to us. We talked every few days. She sent me updates on prenatal visits and I checked in to see how her day at work went. I loved her instantly and no matter what decision she would make nothing could change that.

On August 5th, we made plans to meet for lunch. Zach and I arrived at the restaurant early and waited anxiously in our car. I texted Sydney to let her know we were there and asked her to let me know when she arrived. I knew she was bringing her grandmother and aunt, but other than that I had no idea what she looked like or what kind of car to be on the lookout for. I remember Zach taking my hands and praying in the parking lot as we waited. His prayer eased my nerves slightly, but I don't think anything could remove the nerves completely. The next 15 or so minutes seemed to pass by like slow pouring molasses. The anticipation and jitters grew with every passing second. And then, I spotted them in the distance—or at least I thought I did. Three women stepped out of the car and headed into the restaurant, and we followed a few feet behind. When we stepped inside, I timidly approached the girl. "Are you Sydney?" I asked. Sure enough, it was her. I went in, uncertain if she wanted a hug or handshake, and to my surprise, she extended her arms and we had our first embrace.

The waiter seated us quickly and we all exchanged small talk around the table. The aunt and I both shared similarities of a love of crafting and grandma and I were proud of how much we loved to yard sale and find a good deal. Sydney and I both ordered the same meal and we all made fun of Zach and Sydney for not liking any food on their plates to touch. The conversation flowed and before I knew it, the waiter was handing us the bill. I hated for our afternoon to end, but I was so thankful for the opportunity to meet her and her family. Sydney exuded sarcasm, funny and sweet all in one. As I hugged her goodbye, I hated for her to be in this situation. She didn't seem burdened with pain on the outside, but I couldn't imagine what was going through her mind on the inside. I prayed that it wouldn't be our last encounter.

We continued to text on and off and then on the morning of August 13th, she texted me: "...baby boy should be here today. Happy Monday!"

I immediately called Zach at work and we were off to the hospital. My mind raced the entire drive. I cried happy tears filled with anticipation of holding this precious boy and tears of grief and guilt as I tried desperately to put myself in Sydney's shoes.

If there is another way God, let it be so. I don't want to see her hurting.

I felt conflicted in that moment, like my heart was being pulled apart. I loved this little baby already. I saw him in our family pictures, running down our hallway, and splashing in bubble baths before bedtime. But I loved Sydney equally. I knew my joy would only come through her grief.

A nurse handed me my hospital band and showed me the way to Sydney's room. With each step, I knew in the back of my mind that nothing was final. I knew very well that she could change her mind. But whatever decision she made wouldn't change the love I had for her and this little boy. I knocked on the door and heard a faint, "Come in." Sydney laid in the bed filling out paperwork, grandma rocked her great grandson and auntie sat right beside her with *The Fresh Prince of Bel-Air* reruns playing on the TV behind her. A beautiful picture of love. Grandma immediately offered for me to hold him, but in that moment, I knew my time could wait. Their time was potentially fleeting. I told her he looked so cozy in her arms I wouldn't want to disrupt him. She smiled as she looked back down at him and continued to rock him peacefully.

I may not have a physical copy or picture in hand, but that moment is permanently etched in my memory. Four generations of love. A family who stood together. A moment that, without a doubt, held great pain. But no amount of pain could break their bond. Sydney had support and love and she exemplified bravery.

As the evening progressed, Sydney's family went home with plans to return in the morning. The nurses set up a room for Zach and I just a couple doors down from Sydney's. After all of us had a chance to eat some dinner, Sydney invited us into her room with the baby[3].

---

3. Some events and conversations from this time are left out, out of respect and privacy for everyone involved. I will say, our time was precious and sweet as we shared more about one another's lives and had many opportunities to laugh (mostly at the expense of one incompetent nurse and Sydney's sarcastic wit to narrate the whole situation).

Her baby slept in our room all night. His bassinet stood at my bedside and I fed and cared for him around the clock. When morning came, Sydney texted me to ask if she could have some time alone with him to say her goodbyes. My answer was an emphatic *yes*, she didn't even have to ask. I knew how important this time was for him and her to share. A nurse came to my room almost immediately to bring him to her and Zach and I sat in an empty hospital room that felt as if the walls were closing in on us with every second that passed by.

I wanted Sydney to have this time with him. I truly did. She needed this time with him. She deserved this time with him. But for the next several hours, radio silence was all Zach and I received. My mind wouldn't stop replaying the events of just a few weeks before.

Is Sydney having second thoughts?

My mind prepared my heart to be happy if she did.

A family will be restored! This child will be with his mother!

But my heart had a hard time taking the advice from my mind. I had rocked this baby to sleep. I had felt his heart beating against mine. My whole being already loved him as my son.

Just then, we heard a knock on the door. My heart sank in preparation for who may be waiting on the other side of the door and what news they would bring. I went to open it and saw Sydney's frail and small grandmother standing to greet me on the other side. She walked in our room, looked up at me with tears in her eyes and opened her arms to hug me. Then she reached out and grabbed Zach's hand and pulled him in to give him a hug as well. As the three of us embraced, she shared some parting words of love and gratitude with us. And it was only then, in that moment, that I knew Sydney had gone through with the adoption plan. Joy instantly filled my heart with the realization that we would be bringing this sweet boy home as our son, but I also felt an accompanying heartache for the grieving and loss I could only imagine Sydney was experiencing down the hall. With tears in all our eyes, she walked back out the door and we parted ways. As much as I loved this baby boy, I loved Sydney just as much. And I was so thankful for the opportunity to love her family through this intricate and tangled sorrow and joy filled journey of adoption.

Lord, don't let that be our last embrace. Hold Sydney in the palm of Your hand. Bring her comfort beyond any human understanding right now.

We chose the name Jaxon Korbyn. Jaxon means: God is gracious. And after an agonizing five month span involving a miscarriage, an adoption match that fell through, and now this new baby entering our family we felt God's grace in a very special way. We knew we served a Good Father, but through the ups and downs of the past few months, it was more clear than ever before that God was the one writing our story and He was for us, not against us. He was gracious in our prior losses, and He remained gracious in the birth of this sweet baby boy and we wanted his name to be a reminder of that. Like we did with Jayden, we used the name his birth mother chose for his middle name. A few days later, I shared this post to our Adoption Facebook page:

> Over the past week there have been too many blessings to count, let alone list on a Facebook post, but we wanted to share the exciting news of the arrival of Jaxon "Jax" Korbyn! Jayden is LOVING being a big brother and can't get enough of his "bubby." We ask that you would continue to lift up his birth mother in your prayers. Love is brave!

3

New Beginnings

O ut with the old, in with the new. The 2020 calendar replaced the scribble-filled one before. Christmas decorations were packed away and my home started to resume some kind of normalcy once again. Our rousing plans for New Years Eve held nothing more adventurous than the average weeknight. For the past few days I had been visiting the restroom frequently. I wasn't drinking any more water than usual, but I found myself urinating around the clock. The only reason this struck me as abnormal was because I had an odd pride about the length of time I could go without having to use the restroom. Some might even call it my secret superpower. Of course, no one ever actually *did* call it my secret superpower, but it was pretty super nonetheless.

Growing up, our family hiked Mt. Katahdin almost every summer. I've been up and down that mountain probably a dozen times. We'd wake up in the wee hours of the morning, make the drive to Acadia National Park, sleep in the van until they opened the front gate and start hiking before the sun even bothered to make an appearance. And we wouldn't make it down the mountain until dinner time. A full day of hiking and constantly staying hydrated, BUT I never once had to find a tree to squat behind. All that to say, the fact that I was going to the bathroom about every ten minutes gave me a reason to question my internal organs. Aside from that, I had no reason to even *think* I was pregnant, but I remembered I had a leftover pregnancy test stashed somewhere in the back of my bathroom closet and decided to give it a whirl. Everything I remembered from my infertility days was how important it was to test first thing in the morning. Since I didn't have any reason to believe I'd get a positive result, I figured I might as well test smack dab in the middle of the afternoon.

Three minutes passed and I grabbed the test nonchalantly. But as I looked closer, much to my amazement, I saw not one, but two pink lines.

Not.

A.

Chance!

I couldn't believe what I held in my hand.

Life couldn't just come to a screeching halt. So, I flushed the toilet, washed my hands, and headed back into the dinning room to clean up lunch. Faces washed, plates put in the sink, diapers changed and babies down for their nap. I plopped myself down on the couch in utter disbelief.

Is this really happening?

I love surprises, I really do, but with this shock, I was about to burst at the seams and I couldn't stand being the only one to know. I grabbed a leftover box from Christmas, and a near empty roll of Christmas wrapping. I threw the pregnancy test in the box and wrapped it up. I knew Zach had a short break and would be home any minute. As soon as he walked in the door, I told him I found one more Christmas gift I had forgotten about for him. Yes, you read that correctly—the middle of the work day, sitting in the middle of our living room floor was where I finally decided to surprise Zach with a pregnancy announcement. Pinterest worthy? I'm guessing not!

Neither of us could begin to imagine how our lives were about to change. Family and friends were floored and so happy for us. We were elated for about a month and then news of the Coronavirus flooded TV screens across America. No one knew for sure what the virus would mean for the world, but everyone had an opinion and those opinions were spewed all over social media. The whole world seemed to go on lockdown. Restaurants shut down, non-essential shops were empty, grocery stores ran on different hours. Milk, meat, and toilet paper were high commodities and nowhere to be found. Kids transitioned to virtual education and most workplaces called for everyone to work remotely. Healthcare providers were burnt out from the influx of COVID-19 cases filling hospital beds. Fear and terror struck most households. And here I was, a couple months pregnant.

Zach took over grocery shopping and my OBGYN strongly encouraged me to stay home and quarantine as much as possible. Stir-crazy kicked in on more than one occasion, but so did sweet, sweet memories. Zach was home much more, and time as a family grew extra special. Unknowns surrounded us, but we were blessed with good health and the unexpected gift of quality time. Zach accompanied me to my first ultrasound and got to see the baby. He wasn't allowed in the office for any of my other visits due to COVID-19 restrictions, so we were so thankful he could be there for the ultrasound.

My pregnancy was relatively uneventful. I had some morning sickness early on, but by the second trimester things seemed to settle down. And aside from massive ankles and feet swelling this baby seemed calm and content. I was rarely bothered with internal kicking and I would wait with anxious anticipation at every appointment for the nurses to hear and confirm a heartbeat.

The year 2020 continued with a bang and a whole lot of pain. Between the rise of the Coronavirus, food shortages and lockdowns, racial inequality, riots, and politics, we were extra grateful for this blessing of new life. Lifelong friends, and even families, were breaking apart over the tension of words spewed, mostly over social media, related to the list above. Much of the rising tension revolved around racial inequality. I could never make sense of the racial injustices that occurred during the 1800s and now, two centuries later, it made even less sense to me why it continued. News story after news story drew attention to injustices right before our eyes. Breonna Taylor, Ahmaud Arbery, and most recently George Floyd—a man taken down by brutal police force resulting in his death. One side hated all police officers, the other side tried to justify his death with the absurd argument that *he got what he deserved* because drugs were found in his system. Both sides were completely unable to reach what, in my mind, was just so simply common sense.

Every human holds certain unalienable rights—rights that *cannot*, under any circumstances, be taken away. These rights are bestowed on Americans as part of The Constitution. No matter the color of one's skin, *every* American is deserving of these rights. And as Christians, we hold an even greater responsibility to defend these rights when we see injustice taking place because we know we are *all* made in the image of our Creator. I've got some more to add on this topic a little later—you can find those thoughts in Chapter 6: This is Adoption.

My mom arrived about a week prior to my due date to spend some time with us and to be available to stay with the boys when I went into labor. Wednesday evening on August 19th, we went to bed like normal. But in the wee hours of the morning I started to feel like something wasn't quite right. I woke up around 1:30am and noticed that my sheets were a little damp. Not eager to strip and remake the bed in the dead of the night, I grabbed a bath towel from my closet, laid it over my side of the bedsheet and hopped back in bed trying not to wake Zach.

It's too soon. I'm not ready.

I got back in bed and pretended everything was normal. Unfortunately, for me, everything wasn't normal and I couldn't sleep. Early contractions started hitting, but still I tried my best to ignore them.

I'm convinced Zach could sleep through an earthquake and not be disturbed, but after several, apparently loud, moans he rolled over to check to see if I was ok. I told him I was fine and to just go sleep on the couch so I wouldn't bother him. Half asleep he stumbled out to the couch and I continued my contractions every few minutes. My moaning must have gotten slightly louder because he came back to the bedroom happily concerned. I realize "happily concerned" is confusing, so let me clarify. He was now wide-eyed and bushy tailed. Realizing I was in pain, he was concerned and wanted to make sure I was ok, but he was now flipping on lights left and right and packing a hospital bag giddy as a schoolgirl. "It's baby time! Let's go. Tell me what you need and I'll pack it."

"No, I'm really fine. I'll try to be quieter. Go back to bed, seriously!" No part of me wanted it to *be time*. A rush of fear enclosed me and I just wanted this all to be a dream. Then, trying to sound like he knew a thing or two, said, "Ok, I'm going to time your contractions." Allowing him to do that was a mistake because my contractions were just under five minutes apart so he had all the proof he needed to drag me to the hospital, kicking and screaming the whole way to the car. I stalled as long as I could, but 5am came around and he forced me out the door. The sun hadn't even come up yet, leaving the sky pitch black. I wasn't noticeably crying, but tears began to fall from my eyes. I was a 30 year old woman, but inside, I was just a scared little girl.

The hospital staff admitted me into the emergency room around 5:30am at only two centimeters dilated.

Two centimeters?! You've got to be kidding me!

I figured maybe not quite ten, but surely nine. My contractions were now every three to five minutes. After lying on the bed for a few hours, a delivery room finally opened up. Around 8am, I moved to the new room, still only two centimeters dilated, but the lab tests returned confirming that my water did, indeed, break at home. Contractions continued to increase in pain and I was, unknowingly, majorly dehydrated. After some time, the anesthesiologist administered an epidural, and instantly I had some type of negative reaction to it. As I sat upright for the epidural, Zach and the nurse held my hands while I leaned into both of them. Once the epidural was placed, the nurse said, "Ok sweetie, you can lie back down now." I had no feeling from my waist down and I looked at both her and Zach and said, "I really don't know if I can do it by myself." The nurse assured me, "I know it feels a little weird right now, but you'll be able to lie down." Having done this probably a thousand times with other women, I figured she knew what she was talking about. She did still gently hold my hand to assist me in laying down, but I instantly fell backwards and wacked my head against the headboard.

Thankfully, it sounds worse than it actually felt. I laughed briefly and assured both her and Zach I was fine. But my shaking persisted and became uncontrollable. And suddenly the machines started sounding. Constant beeping echoed in the room on all monitors. The nurse's face focused intently on the screens, her and Zach's eyes darting from one monitor to the other. Their calm exteriors now veiled concentrated concern. My blood pressure dropped to 73/45 and I became fearful! For the first time, a sense of anxious fear rushed over my calm husband. The epidural wore off after several hours of continued, non-progressing labor, and pain and fatigue simultaneously set up camp in my weary body. Only one anesthesiologist was working this particular shift and he was in a surgery with someone else at the moment. We waited about an hour before he could come down and adjust the dosage and try to solve what was going on with my reactions. He seemed to correct the epidural dosage and I began to stabilize. With everything going on, the doctor warned us of her concern about the baby being under stress with a decelerating heart rate, so she put me on oxygen. Not long after, I developed a fever and the shaking continued. At this point I had been laboring around fifteen hours. The doctor was doing everything in her power to avoid a C-Section, but worried about the baby, she warned me that it may be my only choice.

Hours passed and minutes dragged on. The clock read 9:15pm. After my twenty hours of exhausting labor, and still not fully dilated, the doctor prepped a team for our one shot to try to have a vaginal delivery. With an oxygen mask strapped to my face, I started pushing for an audience of around six people or more. No one knew what state the baby would arrive in, so extra bodies were present and ready to jump in and take over if necessary. My legs were completely numb. Zach held one, while the nurse held the other. With each push I was encouraged and applauded and told I was almost there.

The liars!

The pushing continued for just over an hour, and then with an exploding gush he arrived. Jordan (Jordy) Ryan was born at 10:24pm. Twenty-one long, agonizing hours of labor with every last second absolutely worth it.

For nine months, I had held this baby in my womb. I had caressed him wherever I went, I had prayed for him, I had loved him and had longed to hold him in my arms, and now I finally could. His tiny 7lb 2oz frame lay on my chest and I was left in awe of my God once again.

My fever lingered and antibiotics were not cutting it. About an hour after Jordy was born, a rush of severe pain swept over me. My whole body was in a state of unrest. Jordy needed his first bottle, and my shaking and pain was so intense I thought I would physically drop him if I held him. As heartbreaking as it was to not give him his first feeding, I can look back now and see how special it was for him to get his very first bottle from his daddy.

By this time, Zach and I had both been up for more than 24 hours. Jordy slept in the bassinet snug by my bedside, Zach was out cold on the couch up against the wall with his legs sprawled over the arm, and I was starting to come back to a somewhat "normal" state. At 4am, a nurse came in to escort us to the recovery postpartum room.

To explain the rest of our time in the hospital I have to first explain my husband. The term "sleeps like a rock" could have been invented in his honor. He can sleep through anything—a baby crying right beside his bed, me changing, feeding, and burping a baby lying down next to him. It doesn't matter what it is; he will without a doubt be dead to the world. And lest you are inclined to assume, "Oh, that's a classic case of selective hearing," let me just assure you, it isn't! I genuinely would fear for his life if there was ever a fire in our home and I wasn't there to wake him up. He is also the person who awakens abruptly in panic from his sleep from time to time.

Knowing this about my husband still didn't prepare me for his response as we were about to change hospital rooms. Exhausted from being awake for over 24 hours, I was ready to be in a room where I could shut my eyes in peace (as much as possible with nurses coming in around the clock). The nurse helped me use the restroom for the first time postpartum, which was a treat all in itself, and then helped me into the wheelchair. My dear husband was sleeping through all of this, mind you. I didn't have time to unpack my "Hey sweetie honey" loving tone on him, so I very plainly said, "Ok, Zach let's go. You need to get the bags. We're changing rooms." Let me also clarify that since the nurse first walked through the door both of us had been calling his name and telling him it was time to leave, to which we received no response from him. When I realized he was just not going to cooperate, I got out of the wheelchair and went straight to him. Shaking his shoulder rather forcefully I said, "Zach, we really need to go. Get up!" He sprang forward and yelled, "What? What? What's happening?"

Could he be any more embarrassing right now?

I turned to the nurse, "It's ok, he does this sometimes. I'm sorry." I should have known better than to turn around for a millisecond because in that short instant he fell back down and went to sleep again. I shook him once more, "Zach, seriously! Get up! You need to get the bags. The nurse is waiting on us!" And, surprise, surprise, he springs forward in dread and panic yet again pushing me away, "What? Who are you? What?" I locked eyes with him and with a single look I let him know this momma wasn't in the mood to indulge in his sleep tactics so he had better wake up and snap out of it. He did, and proceeded to grab our bags and walk over to me. As I got situated back in the wheelchair for a second time, Zach approached us, *finally*. The nurse lifted Jordy from his bassinet and looked over at Zach smiling, "Do you want to carry your son to the room, dad?" My eyes darted at the nurse and I said, "There's no way he's holding that baby right now. I'll take him, thank you." At this point Zach was with it enough to know how much he *wasn't* with it moments ago, so the three of us had a good laugh on our way to the recovery room. On September 3rd, I posted this to my Author Facebook page announcing Jordan's birth.

Our family has some exciting news to share after a couple months of quiet on this page. I've been hesitant on how to share, or even if I should share at all, but just as I have been open about my sorrows, I want to be open about the JOYS God has graciously bestowed on our family. I realize many women on this page relate on a very personal level with the heartache of infertility, and part of the reason I contemplated sharing this news is that I know how much a birth announcement can sting. I know the struggle with wanting to be happy for someone's news while at the same time reading every line of the announcement with tears coming down your face. And if that is you right now, know you are not alone! And know that before I shared this post, I prayed for YOU!

What came as a complete surprise to our family was orchestrated long ago by God. We're thankful to announce the arrival of our baby boy... Jordan "Jordy" Ryan born August 20. We chose the name Jordan because of how the Jordan River is associated with new beginnings in the Bible. Joshua led the nation of Israel across the Jordan to enter the promised land and Jesus began His earthly ministry following his baptism in the Jordan. The Jordan River also played a significant role in Elijah and Elisha's ministry, in the healing of Naaman, and in many other places. We are so thankful for this sweet "new beginning" in our family!

4

God is Deliverance

April 1, 2021, the day of all jokes, had arrived. One hard-working husband and father, three boys with no lack of energy and one very tired wife and momma. If there was one parenting *win* Zach and I had implemented in our family it was that our boys had an early bedtime. When 7:30pm rolled around they were bathed, dressed, and tucked in bed. This allowed Zach and I to have the evening together, a special uninterrupted time for just him and me. This day was particularly long. You know how the saying goes, "The days are long but the years are short"? I was particularly feeling *the days are long* portion of that saying and, to say the least, we were both wiped out. The bedtime routine that usually went off without a hitch lingered. One boy cried, another one wanted water, and one continued to sneak out to the stairway thinking he might get lucky and skip bedtime altogether tonight. We finally got all three down and sleeping and we flopped, exhausted, on the couch. I laid my head on Zach's chest and started laughing. Nothing at all was funny about tonight, but for some reason *slap happy* got the best of me. "Want to do this all over again?" I asked him.

"Ha. Good one," he replied, rolling his eyes.

"I know it's April Fool's and this will go down in history as the worst way to tell you, but after the night we've had, I figured I might as well come right out and say it."

"Stop, Leeann. You're pregnant? No. You're joking." He fumbled as if he could somehow backtrack and change the facts of science now.

"I seriously am. I took a test this morning," I assured him.

"Oh, Leeann. What did we do? We were not responsible. What did we do?"

Realizing he was actually speaking these words, out loud, to his newly pregnant and hormonal wife, he realized he had better throw in a few positives.

"I'm happy. I really am. Babies are a blessing. This was not responsible. Babies are a blessing. They really are. I'm very thankful."

Repetitive and fumbled words were all he could seem to utter. The transition to three kids was kicking our butt at a rapid pace. And that was with Jordan as a model baby. He was the definition of a *chill baby*, and everyone agreed. How on earth could we add a fourth to the mix?

Jayden and Jaxon were the first ones we shared the news with, and being the absolute best big brothers they are, they were so excited. "Are you serious? Are you really serious?" they exclaimed with smiles plastered on their faces and giggles echoing through the living room.

Zach and I had been on a list for roughly two years now with a group from our church to go on a trip to Israel, Rome, and Greece. With the Coronavirus on the rise, our trip continued to be postponed and finally canceled due to flight and country regulations. On a spur-of-the-moment-thinking-out-loud-spewing-from-my-mouth whim, I suggested to Zach that we should just go ahead and take a trip with the airline credit that was about to expire. We knew in a matter of months it would be near impossible to pull off a trip just the two of us leaving four young children behind in someone else's care.

In a matter of days our trip destination went from New York City to California to Europe or maybe Italy at an uncomfortable but exciting and rapid pace. We were acting as if the options were endless. And, in a way, they were. The airline credit from the Israel trip was nearing an expiration date and we didn't want our money to go to waste, so we had a pretty much open map of destinations.

Were we being too whimsical about it all? Could we really take a trip of a lifetime? Now? Five months pregnant?

The next day Zach suggested Iceland.

Eh, I was thinking more Eiffel Tower, rowing in a Gondola kinda thing, actually.

But I entertained the idea anyway. Over the next few days we both did our own personal research of Iceland and wondered how this country was never on our bucket list to begin with. Iceland looked incredible! For the next several weeks I researched "must sees" and sample itineraries. I spent hours during the boys' rest time and late into the evenings putting together an itinerary that included a plethora of amazing places to visit and explore. We booked airline tickets, seven different AirBnbs around the south eastern perimeter of Iceland, a rental car secured for ten days, two different excursions, and a list of places to visit and explore every day. We learned in our research that Iceland was an expensive place to visit, and since we were allowed to each take one checked bag for free, I devoted one piece of luggage entirely to food. Since our days would be full of driving and sightseeing, I knew I could save money by packing breakfast and lunches to go and we could picnic in the car. Zach's parents graciously agreed to stay with our boys for the time we were away, and I knew I had nothing to worry about while they were in Memaw and Grandpa's care. I created small daily gifts for the boys to open each day, and the boys and I created some construction paper chains to countdown the days until we returned.

Upon landing in Iceland, we rented a car from the airport and took off. We didn't make it maybe five minutes down the road before we saw wild horses and sheep grazing just a few feet from our car. My husband, who isn't normally pro-picture taking, was a whole new man in Iceland and, upon his suggestion, we pulled over immediately to snap a picture. The entire route of our itinerary was constantly interrupted by pulling over to the side of the road to soak in the majestic views. Living in the same home and neighborhood day after day, it's easy to become accustomed to God's beautiful creation surrounding you and take it for granted, but in Iceland, God's creation was brilliant and new and on full display every second of every day. From sunrise to sunset we were in awe of the beauty surrounding us. We hiked three volcanoes, one of which was currently erupting and from a distance we were able to see the lava spewing out. We hiked behind waterfalls and into a cave to see a hidden waterfall, held broken pieces of glaciers floating down to the ocean, visited a secret hot spring in the middle of a wide open field, hiked around a canyon and crater, took a ferry to a remote Island, explored erupting geysers, hiked to a lighthouse to see puffins up close, and explored the streets of downtown Reykjavik, Iceland's capital.

The time we spent just Zach and me (and our fourth child growing inside me) was such a treasured time. It was a time I will cherish the rest of my life. Not just because Iceland is an amazing place to explore, but because I was exploring this new destination with my one and only. For the past five years, our time and attention mostly revolved around tiny hands to hold, tiny mouths to feed, and tiny, but demanding, little boys to provide for. And boy did I love providing and caring for those growing little boys, but I missed the *man* who stole my heart nine years before they ever entered the picture. And in those ten days, I fell in love all over again.

By the end of our getaway though, we were both ready to be home to our babies. Evening Facetime calls weren't cutting it anymore. We both needed the real life, in person, big bear hugs and slobbery kisses back. As much as the peace and quiet was a nice change of pace, we needed the endless questions from curious toddlers, sticky counter-tops, and sweet voices telling us *I love you!* We missed our babies and we couldn't wait to be in the same zip code as them once again!

The honeymoon portion of my pregnancy came to a screeching halt and my third trimester arrived with a bang. The pregnancy with this baby was becoming very different from my pregnancy with Jordan. With this pregnancy, I was uncomfortable daily. I constantly felt worn out and wasted. I got sick more often and from the third trimester until delivery time, sleep was just something I couldn't get. I'd be up in the middle of the night mentally and physically exhausted but my body couldn't seem to shut down and find rest. Everyone would come up to me asking, "How are you feeling?" and quite frankly, I got tired of giving the *glass half full* answer of, "Great!" So, slowly my answer seemed to morph into, "I'm hanging in there. We're on the home stretch." One of my friends came up to me in church one morning and said, "Wow, you look like you could have this baby any day now." At that point, I still had a good month or two to go. My whole body just screamed, *are we there yet?*

My in-laws arrived in town Thursday afternoon on November 4th. They planned for a long weekend trip to celebrate Jayden's birthday on the 9th. I've never been more excited to see my mother-in-law, because her presence meant *help*, and help was exactly what I needed. She walked through the door and sat down next to me on the couch.

She barely got a chance to greet her grandsons and she put her hand on my leg and said, "Oh, Leeann. You look so tired. You need to get some rest while I'm here."

Exhaustion was written all over my face. My in-laws were here through the weekend and I took full advantage of an extra set of eyes watching my babies so I could catch a few catnaps during the day. I blinked and it was now Tuesday, November 9th, Jayden's fifth birthday!

Five!

How is he already five?

I drove him to school in the morning and dreaded the nearing of the afternoon because it meant my help was catching a flight back to Florida. My in-laws were packed and dropped off at the airport and I was back in the car, this time returning with Jayden from his school day. His birthday gifts were all wrapped and set up on the dining room table waiting for him to open after his last flag football game of the season. It was a jam-packed day, but I was excited to celebrate my boy.

We had been home about an hour by now. Jayden and Jaxon were watching a show on TV and I was preparing an early supper before his football game. I felt an urge to go to the bathroom, but I didn't make it in time!

Not this again!

I finished peeing (or thought I did, anyway) and got up only to feel another cascade. Confident that I really had mastered potty training way back when, paranoia began to set in. My water breaking was the only logical explanation, but it was too early. The baby couldn't come this soon. In tears I called Zach who was working only a few minutes away. "It can't be my water breaking, but I don't know what else it could be. It's way too soon for my water to break."

"It's baby time!" was the first thing out of his mouth. He didn't share in my anxiety. In fact, he reveled in it. He did give me the intelligent advice to call my doctor *(why didn't I think about that?)* but in his mind, his work day was done and we were going to skip right on over to the hospital.

By this time, my in-laws were already checked into their flight and at their gate ready for boarding. The timing of my water breaking could not be more inconvenient if it was written for an Oscar Award winning comedy:

- My in-laws were at the airport after staying for five days and planning to return December 1st (eight days prior to my original due date—just in case the baby decided to come early).

- Today was Jayden's birthday.

- Jayden had his last flag football game.

- Jayden hadn't opened any of his birthday gifts yet.

- My due date was still a month away.

- I was running out of clothes because my water kept *breaking* through all my outfit changes.

As I stood frozen on a towel in my bathroom crying, Jayden hesitantly peeked in to see what was wrong with his lunatic mother. "Why are you crying mommy?"

"Because I think it might be time for me to have the baby. I'm so sorry, baby. I don't want to ruin your birthday."

"Wait! You're going to have the baby now? But it's not Christmas yet!" The only way to put an end to the ceaseless questioning of when I was going to have the baby was to keep telling the boys the baby would come at Christmas. My due date was December 8th, so *Christmas time* seemed like an appropriate answer to provide them with.

Jayden was ecstatic, which only made my emotions bubble over more.

He would be ecstatic. That's just like him. Leave it to Jayden to not be phased at all by missing out on his birthday celebrations to welcome a new baby into our family. He was made to be a big brother.

I heard the back door burst open with Zach yelling, "Is it baby time in here?" So of course, that prompted me to soak my face in a fresh batch of tears.

Why not, I was already soaking up the bath towel with my water breaking every five seconds, might as well soak up my face at the same time.

Zach met me in the bathroom, scooting around with a towel underfoot. I had no idea where to even start packing a hospital bag. So, instead, I just kept pacing, really *scooting* in circles around the bathroom floor. We chose to be surprised by the gender again, so I also didn't have a clue what to pack for a baby. I stood there, completely vulnerable, crying and apologizing over and over for ruining Jayden's birthday. As I stood there crying, Zach was simultaneously calling his parents from the airport to see if they had taken off yet. He caught his mom minutes before she scanned her ticket to enter the jet bridge.

Praise God!

Meanwhile, I'm still scooting around, useless to everyone around me, still trying to figure out what to pack in a hospital bag, with nothing yet successfully *in* the hospital bag. *One would think I hadn't done this three times before.*

By this time, I had contacted my doctor and was given the go-ahead to admit myself into the hospital. Contractions had started but I wasn't anywhere close to a ten on the pain scale, so I told Zach we could pick up his mom from the airport on our way so she didn't have to get an Uber. We hopped in the van, boys giggling and laughing in the back seat as they got buckled, and Zach taking a minute to video document our drive before actually hitting the road. Jayden's guess was a girl, yet he still wanted the name Joshua *so I'm not quite convinced he fully thought it was a girl*. Jaxon's response was "two," to which Zach replied, "Oh, boy! It better not be two!"

The airport was only a few minutes from the hospital, but my labor decided it would be fun to play a trick on me and occur during rush hour, so the drive took probably double what it should have.

We finally arrived at the hospital, and my big ol' belly and I crawled to the backseat so I could give my boys a hug and kiss good-bye. Zach grabbed the hospital bag and infant car seat and we waved goodbye as Memaw drove off to grab a bite to eat with the boys.

The hospital staff admitted me pretty quickly and I soon found out my doctor was on call. A sense of relief fell over me. Over the past few years I had grown a great relationship with her. She, unfortunately, had to deliver the infertility news, along with the miscarriage news a couple years later, but she was also the one to confirm a normal, healthy pregnancy in both Jordan and this little baby. She and her husband had also adopted, and we both shared the same faith in our unwavering God. I had grown to love her as a friend and not just as the OBGYN I saw every few weeks. After several minutes of uncomfortable question-answering from the nurse, in between progressively more painful contractions, in walked my doctor, and I had never been more happy to see her.

"What are you doing here?" she smiled.

"I have no idea!" was my very honest response back. I still couldn't believe I was in the hospital, in labor, a month early, on Jayden's birthday.

The minutes ticked by and my labor this time around seemed to be going much more smoothly than it had with Jordan. Minutes turned to hours and it was now nearing midnight. Around 11pm I started feeling a pressure that was so persistent I called for the nurse. She took one look at me and said, "It's baby time, mamma!"

My doctor quickly assembled a whole team in case this baby needed to be rushed to the NICU. Once again, much like with Jordan, I had an entire room full of people as an audience to my pushing. Most of it is a complete blur to me, but *thankfully* I have my wonderful husband to remind me that he's never seen a face get as red as mine when I'm giving birth.

What a lovely picture to be printed in my mind, and now yours, probably forever. Thank you, Zach.

After only about five pushes, sweet baby made an appearance. The cord that was wrapped around its neck was quickly cut and my doctor looked up at Zach and asked, "You want to announce the gender, dad?"

"It's another boy!" he smiled as he cut the cord and leaned down to kiss my forehead.

Our boy, our fourth precious baby boy, was immediately placed on my chest and all sense of pain left my body and was instantly replaced with a sweeping relief. He was a healthy 6lb 1oz boy and didn't need a single second in the NICU. Thirty-five weeks and six days with twenty-nine minutes to spare. Born at 11:31pm, he just barely made it in time to share a birthday with his big brother. The next morning, we posted this to our Facebook announcing his birth.

Well, yesterday's birthday celebrations for our big five year old went a little differently than expected. The original due date for our 4th was supposed to be December 8th, however sweet boy had a mind of his own and decided to make an early appearance and share a birthday with big brother.

For months now, Jayden has wanted the new baby to be named Joshua. Joshua is his favorite hero of the faith, and he loves reading any Bible story featuring Joshua. The name means "God is deliverance". Joshua wasn't on our list of potential names prior to going into delivery, but as the labor went on and when he was finally placed in our arms we knew that was his name. A very special birthday gift to his big brother (who truly picked out his brother's name—not many 5 year olds can say that) and also a reminder to us all every time we say his name, of our great God using Joshua to lead His chosen people into the promised land. And an even bigger reminder of our Heavenly Father who sent his Son, the ultimate deliverer of the World. Welcome to the world, Joshua Judah!

On November 12th, our bags were packed and we were on our way out of the hospital. We took a left out of our room, down a long hallway and onto the elevator. As we exited the elevator doors, I glanced over to the waiting area—the same waiting area where Zach and I had sat just three years prior for the adoption match that ended in unification for the mother and her child.

Three years ago, the waiting area felt cold and seemed dim. The faith I had in my good and gracious Father was beginning to blossom, but only through deep anguish. The people walking in and out of the waiting area three years ago wore smiles and cradled babies in their arms. I sat empty-armed and gutted. A baby, one whose name I will never know, was born to a woman who had lost all hope. But because of the love for her child, she found the strength to not place him for adoption, but instead to raise him herself. Three years ago I had rejoiced in the beauty of unification for this mother and her son and I had wept over the loss of a relationship I envisioned us all having. In the same hospital I, a woman with an infertility diagnosis, had now given birth twice. Two adoptions, one miscarriage, two pregnancies, resulting in four babies to a *mother*, a name I had feared I would never own.

I cradled my fourth child in my arms while being wheeled out of the hospital. It was the same waiting room that had once left me feeling broken. The same speaker system resounded with the same calls paging for medical staff, and the same muffled chatter echoed from friends and family pacing the floors. The same expired magazines were stacked on the end tables next to the same blue vinyl chairs. Everything looked the same, as if nothing at all had changed. And then I felt a rush of God's favor over my life. Countless times He has walked with me. Countless times He has carried me. Through my suffering, He went before me and never once abandoned me even when my faith proved small. He took my hopes and dreams, fears and failures, and created a masterpiece I never knew I wanted, but couldn't imagine my life without. And I realized, in that moment, that *everything* had changed. Maybe not the walls, or the chairs or the call signals, but everything that mattered had changed. This room once felt like a field of brokenness, but I could see now how God had been crafting beauty through all of the pain. God was continually reshaping my broken pieces to reflect His own glory.

Part Two:
Looking Ahead

Since then we have a great high priest who has passed through the heavens, Jesus, the Son of God, let us hold fast our confession. For we do not have a high priest who is unable to sympathize with our weaknesses, but one who in every respect has been tempted as we are, yet without sin. Let us then with confidence draw near to the throne of grace, that we may receive mercy and find grace to help in time of need.

(Hebrews 4:14-16)

5
Hands Full

◇

I pushed my cart full of children and groceries to my mom-mobile, sporting the fashionable messy bun and t-shirt look that seemed to accompany me everywhere. I wore Joshua in my boba wrap, Jordan and Jaxon shared the front seat of the cart, and Jayden walked beside me, holding on to the cart. I had just finished unbuckling and unwrapping the last child and re-buckling them into car seats when I started to unload the bags of groceries.

"I will never again complain about taking one kid to the grocery store. That was impressive," yelled a woman from the next row over in the parking lot.

I looked over, frantically retracing my steps in my mind to decipher if I had done anything foolish on my walk to the car before I realized I had an audience. Just as I was about to give myself the proverbial pat on the back for my "impressive" mom job, a random bottle fell out of my bag and rolled deep under the van. I knelt down on all fours, squashing my pride while doing so, to reach far behind the back tire and grab it.

"Either crazy or impressive, depending on how you look at it I guess. Have a good one," I laughed and yelled back, waving goodbye.

Isn't that how it always seems to go? Just when you think you've reached superstar mom status (honestly, do we ever really feel *that* high?) we are brought down to earth—sometimes literally—with any signs of pride washed away.

"Boy, you have your hands full" is a phrase I hear almost every time I am out in public with my boys. They aren't wrong. When I'm out, alone with the boys, my hands are either full of babies, full of groceries, or something related to either of those two things. When I'm home, you can tell from my dish-filled sink, toy-scattered floor, and laundry basket piled high with clothes that my hands are pretty full no matter where I am. After the fact, I always wish I had some type of quick response to that statement. Yes, the statement is true, but somehow it always seems to come across as a negative rather than a positive. There's the, "If you think my hands are full you should see my heart" reply, but I haven't yet been successful at uttering that response in real-life situations, just in my head. So here is what I wish I could say to all the strangers who have decided I am the poster child for the *hands full* statement.

Yes, you are right. Everyone is right. My hands are so full that I often dream up an imaginary nanny that accompanies us on errand day. Actually, since I'm dreaming, I might as well dream big. She doesn't just accompany me, she does it *all* for me. I don't even have to tag along. She then magically flies home before I arrive and has my house in tip-top shape. You can almost see clean sparkles appearing out of thin air. No socks are without a partner and door handles have no sticky residue from a PB&J lunch three days prior. There isn't a layer of dust on the top of the ceiling fan blades and baseboards, and a nice hot meal is baking in the oven with a tossed salad all prepped in the refrigerator.

This magical, imaginary nanny sounds wonderful at first, but with her, I miss out on so much of the mundane life that is essential for growing our family. The magical nanny doesn't teach my boys the responsibility of helping unload the dishwasher and learning to work together to accomplish a task that helps serve someone else. The magical nanny doesn't remind my boys to act respectfully when we walk through a store to make sure they are setting a good example with their testimony to others around them. The magical nanny doesn't allow my boys to use their imagination as they play with toys all throughout the house.

I remember the first time I took Jayden shopping by myself to the grocery store. He was my only child at the time, and I was terrified for the two of us to attempt this seemingly daunting task.

What if he cried while we were shopping? What if he had a messy diaper?

I would bring his diaper bag into the store with us for fear that in the 30 minutes of shopping he would surely need something from that bag. With every child that was added I worried less about the *daunting task* ahead and rather just grew accustomed to it instead. The reaction I normally get when someone finds out I shop with all the boys is one of shock and amazement. And if you would have asked *mother of one* Leeann, that's definitely the response she would have given too. Somehow though, after baby two, three, and four, it just somehow became *normal*. And *normal* is the kind of life I want with my boys. Not everyone else's version of *normal*, but our very own, copyrighted version of *Hale Normal!* Call me crazy, but I genuinely enjoy doing life side-by-side-by-side-by-side with my boys.

Now, real mom talk. Are there days that I feel I'm about to lose the only bit of sanity I have left if I have to break up another argument, change another diaper, or fold another load of laundry? One hundred times *yes!* I'm not even remotely close to the glorified, figmented Super-Mom status (and I personally know some of those moms, so trust me when I say, *that ain't me, sister!*). I'm ashamed to say there are probably more minutes of my day that resemble utter exhaustion than blissful joy. In this season of life, my focus is to push through the extreme hard because I know that the next season of life is coming where I can reap the joy of the seeds that I've worked so hard to sow. The future season now seems so distant and far off, but at times I can envision small shadowy glimpses. I see toddlers turned to teenagers who turn to adult men. Tiny bouncy balls the size of my hand turn to Friday night home games and championships. Endless kisses from a toddler who has eyes for only mommy turn into first dates and mother son dances at their wedding (currently Jayden has agreed to dance to "Ain't No Mountain High Enough" with me and Jaxon's choice is "I Like to Move it Move it" from the Madagascar movie. Here's to hoping Jaxon finds a new favorite for us before his wedding day otherwise those are going to be three very humbling minutes of dancing for this mother of the groom).

Let me encourage you where you are today. Whether you're zombie-ing through the around the clock feedings or your last baby has just left the nest, rest in this: Jesus can relate! Hebrews 4:14-16 says, "Since then we have a great high priest who has passed through the heavens, Jesus, the Son of God, let us hold fast our confession. For we do not have a high priest who is unable to sympathize with our weaknesses, but one who in every respect has been tempted as we are, yet without sin. Let us then with confidence draw near to the throne of grace, that we may receive mercy and find grace to help in time of need."

Jesus faced utter exhaustion. Jesus felt the shun of being an outsider. Jesus suffered unjust punishment. But the difference between Him and us is that He faced those trials PERFECTLY! Because of our fallen sin nature, there is no way we can face our trials with perfection. But we can face them with the *One* who holds perfection, our Holy High Priest, our Righteous Judge, Our Good Father, our Savior. Life without Him is completely possible. Many have done it before me, and many will do it long after I'm gone. Life without God is *possible*, but it's *not* purposeful.

I've had the opportunity to talk to many women since sharing our story, whether on podcasts, in conversations with friends who just want to know more, or with total strangers who have reached out for comfort and advice as they face similar trials. One of the questions I receive most often is: *How did you make it through?* There is no way to answer that question apart from my Heavenly Father.

There is no way I could have suffered my years of infertility apart from God.

There is no way I could have mourned a miscarriage apart from God.

There is no way I could have journeyed through our adoptions apart from God.

There is no way I could have given birth to two children apart from God.

When I look at my life and all God has blessed me with, I see pain with purpose. I vividly remember my suffering like it was yesterday. And I'm thankful for that because it allows me to be relatable with women walking a similar path. But now that I am out the other side, I can see that pain turned into beauty and I can rejoice in the pain because I know now that it carried great purpose.

Without the pain, I don't think I would have the appreciation I do now. I learned great lessons in my pain. I experienced great growth in my pain. Good gifts came as a result of pain. And although I wouldn't choose to go back and live those days over again, I hope, given the opportunity, that I would glean even more knowledge and a greater love for my Savior than I did the first time around.

If you are walking through the *pain* phase of your journey right now, may I say with all sensitivity, *praise God!* Don't let this time of pain be wasted. Come to the throne of grace where you can find mercy and grace for whatever you are going through. Cry out to the One who can restore you. He has a plan for your life. He knows you and He knows your purpose. The same one whose dwelling place is Heaven is reaching down to comfort *you!* When no one else sees your tears, He wipes away each one that falls. When you feel like you have gone too far astray and can't possibly be loved by anyone, let alone a Holy God, He *welcomes* you to a seat at his table. You are never too far gone for God's mercy to reach out and pull you in.

6
This is Adoption

Time kept ticking as our family kept growing. Christmas morning of 2021, vanished in a blink. All the preparations to make the day special came to a halt in a matter of minutes it seemed. The older boys echoed excited laughter, Jordan was tearing already torn wrapping paper like his one job in life was "Master Shredder," and Joshua rocked away contently in his swing. Jayden's most unrivaled gift of the morning was a five dollar orange trucker hat, and Jaxon beamed with enthusiasm as he opened one dollar bills in a card from his great grandparents.

Christmas has always been one of my favorite days of the year. It reminds me of so many special and treasured moments from my childhood. Christmas Eve was the night it all started. Grammie and Papa Dale hosted a beautiful Christmas Eve evening from start to finish. I always begged my parents to let me go early so I could help prepare the meal. As a girl, this dinner seemed like one from a fairy tale. Cheese fondues with special dipping forks for our homemade Rye Bakery rolls, savory beef tips cooked in a tangy sweet and sour sauce, shrimp dangling off the rim of fancy glasses filled with cock-tail sauce, and fancy wine goblets to hold our sparkling apple cider. After dinner, my brother and I would sort the gifts and then we all took turns going around the circle opening one gift at a time. We always stayed late into the evening and then headed back home to get some sleep before the magic started all over again Christmas morning. Nanny and Granddad arrived for Christmas morning breakfast followed by presents from them and mom and dad in the living room.

Through the years I have memories of watching old home videos of Christmases past, and playing in the background of one of the videos is the song, "Have Yourself a Merry Little Christmas." It's my favorite Christmas song to this day. Not really because of the words—there are far better Christmas lyrics in my opinion—but because of the memories the song holds for me. When I hear that song, I'm nine years old again in my childhood home on Wilson Street. Snow is falling outside. My mom and dad are on the couch watching us tear through all the gifts, and my grandparents are watching right along with them. If there was a time machine that could instantly bring you back to a moment when all seemed right in the world it would be that moment.

The boys were happy as could be and our sweet little family of six was beginning to make memories of our own that I hoped they would look back on one day with the same joy as I look back on mine. I texted Sydney to wish her a Merry Christmas and sent our love along with a few pictures from the morning. We always exchanged texts on the holidays and throughout the year sporadically just to check in. When Jaxon took his first steps, right after Zach, she was the first person I texted. I couldn't wait to tell her! So wishing her a Merry Christmas wasn't anything out of the ordinary for us. She sent a couple updated pictures of herself for us to show Jaxon. He was so proud of any picture he had of his birth mom. When people visited our home he immediately took them to the fridge and pointed to her picture and said, "That my birth mom."

Jayden came over to look at the pictures she texted and so innocently asked, "Did my birth mom send you a picture too?" If ever there was a time I wanted to have a different answer to give my boy it was now. It felt as if my heart had just shattered into a million pieces.

"No, baby. She didn't, but we have a really nice picture of your birth mom and dad on the fridge right here, remember?" Trying to focus his attention on the one picture I had of them I continued, "I love this picture of them. Isn't it such a nice picture? Look at her beautiful smile." He was quickly able to move on and divert his attention. "Yeah, that's a good picture." Then his eyes darted to the string of pictures directly to the right of that picture. A string of pictures from each sport's season of him and Jaxon.

"Look how little I was when I first played soccer. Look at Jaxy. He's a goofball in that picture." Jayden had instantly moved on. I, however, had not.

Why hadn't his birth mom reached out? Does she know we love her? Does she think she would be a bother if she reached out now, after all these years? Are she and her family safe? Healthy?

I walked back to our bedroom. The boys were busy racing their new remote control cars all over the living room and kitchen floors. No one even noticed I disappeared for a moment. I sat down in the back of our walk-in closet as tears ran down my face. I wanted so badly to text her. All I wanted to do was wish her and her family a Merry Christmas. I didn't want her to think we had forgotten about her, or that we didn't care about her. I wanted her to know she could always reach out to us. I wanted her to know how smart Jayden was. I wanted to tell her every milestone he breezed through, how he was a star on the soccer field and the sweetest friend to the kids in his Pre-K class. I wanted to tell her how much he loved Jesus. How he has memorized story after story from God's Word and is truly learning to hide His Word in his heart. I just wanted her to know he was safe and loved beyond words. And I wanted her to know I loved her too and I hadn't once forgotten about her.

As I was having a moment on the floor of the closet, Zach walked in. I knew what his answer would be, but I quickly prayed a silent prayer that today it would be different. "Do you think it would be ok if I texted her? It's been five years. Chances are, she probably has a different number anyway, but do you think it would be bad if I just tried?" I asked in desperation.

"Leeann, I know you mean well and I know your intentions are all great, but I just feel like maybe there's a reason she hasn't reached out in all this time. I would hate for us to reach out and stir up a whole bunch of painful memories for her, ya know? You can do what you want, I trust you. I just think we really need to be careful and respect her wishes with this. We made it very clear that we would always welcome communication from her," he responded.

I knew he was right, but I wanted so badly for him to be wrong. "I just want her to know we love her and we haven't forgotten about her," I sobbed. Knowing he wasn't prepared for a Christmas morning meltdown from the only other adult in the home when he walked in our bedroom looking for batteries, I wiped my eyes and assured him I was fine and I'd be right out. I wasn't fine. I knew that and so did he, but for the rest of Christmas day I resolved to be *fine*.

Adoption is beautiful, but the beauty is accompanied by hurt. Just because we adopted our boys as infants doesn't mean they won't and haven't already been affected by trauma associated with their story. My boys don't know a time when they didn't know they were adopted, partly because our family design makes it glaringly obvious, but also because we've made a point to always be open about their story. We want them to know who they are, where they came from, and that God created them for a divine purpose. At an early age they have had to encounter the mystery of God's sovereignty. As toddlers, both of our boys have expressed the sadness of missing their birth mother or at times having to settle for "I don't know the answer to that question" when asking more about them.

Do my boys live a deprived life? Quite the contrary. When they are scared, they want *us*. When they are excited about something, they want to tell *us*. When they are shy in an unfamiliar setting, their safe place is with *us*. But at times they still desire to simply *know* their birth parents. So, when they are sad or when I have no answers for their questions we cuddle and pray. The solution sounds trivial, but in fact it's purposeful and beautiful. It provides an opportunity to see grief transformed to peace. We thank God for their birth families and express to God how much we love them. We pray for the safety of their birth families throughout the day wherever they may be. We pray that God would watch over and give them protection. And most importantly we pray they would come to *know* God and *believe* in Him so that even if we never get a chance to see them this side of heaven, we can look forward and rejoice in knowing we can spend eternity with them one day.

The sadness doesn't linger. It lasts only a few minutes at most for them until they are off playing with the next toy, but I know as they grow so will the weight of the unknown.

Saviorism comments directed towards Zach and me of, "Oh, you are so special for adopting them. God bless you," or comments directed at my boys, "Oh, they are so lucky they have you" sound sweet and innocent on the surface but do not accurately portray any of us. Zach and I have never aligned ourselves with the *savior mentality*—the idea that by adopting our boys we somehow became their knight in shining armor to rescue them and give them their "happy ever after." Far from it! In a perfect world, adoption wouldn't need to occur because families would have the resources to care for their babies, and families wouldn't need to be separated at all. Adoption isn't a fertility bandaid for a lack of conceiving naturally on your own. But because we are surrounded by broken people in a broken world this isn't the case. Adoption is beautiful because broken pieces are able to be mended, but my boys aren't "lucky." I believe our God is sovereign and He turned a broken situation into an opportunity to showcase *HIS* glory and *HIS* ultimate saviorship, not ours. My boys are *blessed.* Zach and I are *blessed.* We are blessed because through the brokenness God intervened and intricately wove our families. Two mothers, two fathers and one child wrapped in the arms of a loving Savior. This is adoption.

Just like we are open with their adoption story we are open about our family makeup. As a transracial adoptive family, we face topics of conversation that other families don't. It's not a topic of discussion we wake up to talk about every morning, but it's something we want our boys to feel comfortable discussing. People looking in from the outside may make the (incorrect) assumption that because they are so young they don't yet realize the differences in our skin or that it doesn't cause them to have questions. To that, I would correct them and say we have had conversations since Jayden was old enough to speak. When Jordan was born Jayden wanted to know why Jordan looked like the inside of his hand and not the outside of his hand. Even when talking about himself and Jaxon he notices that one has skin slightly darker than the other. Our boys can use the term "melanin" in an accurate sentence that makes them sound like little men in the backseat of our minivan. *Skin* has given us many opportunities to talk about how wonderful our Creator is. God, in His divine artistry, created us all in different shades of brown. Some darker, some lighter, and every shade in between. Not a single person shares the same exact melanin count.

Our boys know that even mommy and daddy don't have the same color skin. Daddy is darker than mommy and mommy is darker than Joshua. This provides an opportunity to explain that Heaven will have people of every single shade of brown you could ever imagine and that it's neat to think of our family as a very small sample size of Heaven.

Over the years, America has tried to categorize people groups based on skin hue. If one shade is of higher or lower melanin counts, they are labeled with a specific race. However, as believers, it should be especially clear that we are all from *one* race, and *one* blood: "And he made from **one man** *every* nation of mankind to live on all the face of the earth, having determined allotted periods and the boundaries of their dwelling place" (Acts 17:26).

The year 2020 saw a great deal of unrest around these issues of race. The police murder of George Floyd seemed to be a tipping point. Riots broke out in response. Peaceful protests flooded the streets. Black Lives Matter (BLM) signs were raised along with the eyebrows of the average white American family assuming danger was on the prowl. A small subset of people who took full advantage of riots with intent to harm and destroy now somehow became the face of every black person in America. If our country wasn't already proof of The Fall, it sure was now.

My heart ached in ways I couldn't put into words. Friends on Facebook made long arguments and my insides would boil. I'd write a huge, rather aggressive response on my phone only to delete it seconds later without ever posting. There were so many replies I wanted to fire back, but that's exactly what I would have done: *fire* back. I knew my response needed to demonstrate a knees first approach. I needed to begin with prayer. God is a Righteous Judge. He cannot and will not let sin go unpunished, but He also responds in love and commands us to do the same. Matthew 5:44 says, "But I say to you, love your enemies and pray for those who persecute you." I prayed the way I felt would be the same if I didn't have two sons who were of African American descent, but I would never be one hundred percent certain. I lay awake at night thinking about their life and what it would look like when they were teenagers. Adults.

Growing up, Harriet Tubman—often referred to as the Moses of her time—was my favorite person to study. When I was in second grade, my teacher read to us from *Pass It On: African American Poetry for Children* and I had the book memorized practically cover to cover, but the one written about Harriet was always my favorite. As a child, I could never understand why anyone would think it ok to treat someone differently because of the color of their skin. How could *anyone* stand behind the argument that the color of your skin could somehow dictate your worth? I remember reading how Harriet risked her life, time and time again, to bring other slaves to freedom. I stood in awe of her bravery, and still do to this day. The only glimmer of hope from her story, and many like hers, is that it happened in the *past*. The cruelty of one human owning another human being was an event from the *past*; an ugly part of American *history*. So why, in the year of 2020, was America still facing racial injustice? My heart broke, and I knew if mine hurt this much, how much more for my brothers and sisters of color? On June 1st, I posted this to my Facebook:

> It's taken me a while to post something because honestly, I just don't have the words. And if you know me, you know I very much dislike controversy and I know part of what I'm saying won't be understood or agreed upon with everyone. But the amount of time I'm lying awake at night thinking about this subject the more I want to speak up! Not only for

my boys (who will most likely never see this—but does that matter?) but for my fellow black brothers and sisters who are hurting more than I could ever imagine. I'm angry! I'm angry that it's 2020, and we are STILL living in a life where the color of your skin dictates the treatment you receive. I'm angry that I'm raising two young boys who will grow to be black men and will have to think twice before they do simple things like taking an evening jog.

I'm angry that some people were more concerned about Kaepernick's knee than the knee that ended the life of George Floyd. I'm angry that so many peaceful protests went dismissed, unheard, and overlooked leaving people feeling the only option left was escalation since their voices were ignored. Voices that have tried time and time again to defend their rights stated in the Declaration of Independence, "...We hold these truths to be self-evident, that all men are created equal, that they are endowed by their Creator with certain unalienable Rights, that among these are Life, Liberty and the pursuit of Happiness. That to secure these rights, Governments are instituted among Men, deriving their just powers from the consent of the governed..." We are ALL image bearers of God.

As I said before, my boys will most likely never read this. But I pray by the time they can read something like this they will have confidence in knowing that their mother HEARS them, will always HEAR them, and will ALWAYS stand by them! This post won't stop what has been going on for years, and it won't stop what will happen in the future, but what it will do is show that I refuse to be silent. The only thing that will end the hateful hearts that racism stems from is the transformative power of the gospel. To my brothers and sisters who are hurting and feeling unheard right now, I love you and I hear you!

As a transracial family my husband and I carry a big responsibility. It is a responsibility that forces us to step outside our comfort zone and showcase our vulnerability. I remember being a vendor at an adoption conference soon after I published my first book. My books were arranged neatly on the table and a framed family picture stood on display making it very evident that we were a transracial family. Over the course of the weekend, I had many people stop by my booth to talk or purchase a copy of my book, but one lady in particular stood out from the rest. She came over, barely managed to force a smile and said, "You families try to turn these babies white when they're not white." Her comment stung! And, at the risk of sounding like a five year old, I'll tell you the truth: it really hurt my feelings. I was offended that she would place that judgment on me at first introductions. But as more time has passed, I really don't blame her. Unfortunately, far too many transracial families unknowingly, and sometimes knowingly, do exactly what she was warning me against. It's so much easier to raise a child the way you were raised and stay in your lane of ease and comfort. But the child deserves so much more than that.

"Christian technicalities" of proving we don't *deserve* anything aside, the child *deserves* to know where they came from. They *deserve* to not feel like an outsider in their own home and they *deserve* parents who are going to give them the opportunity to learn and feel confident in the man or woman God created them to be. Adopting a child of another race is about loving and exploring their culture and teaching them to do the same. It's a commitment to never stop learning.

Hair is a big part of culture that required—and continues to require—much learning, education, and seeking help on my part. I cut my husband's hair. He hasn't gone to a hair salon since we started dating in college. I've always been a bargain shopper, so even though he successfully asks for a haircut at the most inconvenient times, *every single time*, I still get far too excited about the money we save each time I cut his hair. But Jayden was a different story. As he grew, I didn't want to do anything to mess up his hair. I knew his hair was his crown, and I wanted him to wear it proudly so I proceeded to ask for advice. I sounded stupid on more occasions than I could count, but I wanted to be sure I was respecting him even though he was far too young to care.

As he got older, I wanted him to have the barber shop experience. There was a Great Clips just minutes from our house that would have been a thousand times more convenient to drive to, but that's not where he *deserved* to go. So instead, we drove twenty minutes to the next city over to the barber shop where we first met Ms. Tina. The barber shop was very much outside of my lane of comfort. Everyone who walked into the shop acted like family. They knew *where* to sit and *who* to go to to get a cut that the barber already knew they wanted. I walked in and instantly felt out of place. Jayden was probably two or three years old at the time, and as shy as he is with people he doesn't know, he walked right up to Ms. Tina's chair when she walked over to greet him. In that first meeting they instantly formed a bond. As she was cutting his hair, Jayden kept looking over at his daddy and me with a smirk on his face that let us know he was feeling so important. So proud. So grown.

With each trip to the barber shop, I felt less and less uncomfortable and Jayden felt more and more proud. Ms. Tina didn't just greet me with a hello but with a huge hug and a *How you doin momma? God is so good isn't He? Jayden's my boy. Him and I, we have a bond now. He doesn't want to go to anyone else but me.* And she sure was right.

After Ms. Tina gives him a stylish fresh cut and lets him walk out of the shop with practically her entire drawer of suckers, Jayden gets fist bumps and high fives from all the other guys. They'll stop their cut just to make him feel special. And it doesn't stop there. Ms. Tina walks me over to the hair shop down the sidewalk to help me restock on any hair supplies I may have run out of. More hugs are exchanged and then we're off.

You see, the trip to the barber shop is much more than a twenty minute cut. It's building a family. Jayden is surrounded by an entire shop of people who look just like him. He is loved by an entire shop of people who aren't related to him, but see him as their nephew. The crown on his head is masterfully shaped and he's given several dabs of cologne for the cherry on top. He doesn't walk out on the same pavement as me to the car; he's soaring on the clouds feeling like a million bucks. And I'll tell you one thing, there's no Great Clips in this world that's going to give that to my son, I can guarantee you that!

Hair is only a small part of a much larger picture. Loving Jayden and Jaxon means loving *all* of them. It means educating myself and asking for help when I don't know the answer. During the time of chaos in our country, many churches didn't know how to respond, so sadly, most chose the approach of no response. I was especially thankful for a specific Sunday School class one of the pastors at our church led. He stood before us, upfront and honest, not claiming to have all the answers, but still wanting to open the dialogue and refused to let the circumstances our country was facing be swept under the rug. He spoke on racial injustice and how the only way to begin to fix the problems this world was facing was to go gospel first.

I remember sitting in that Sunday School class with tears running down my cheeks. Yes, I was pregnant and hormonal at the time, but this was so much more than hormones. Every word he spoke, all I could see were the faces of my boys and their futures.

How did we get here? The place where "we don't see color" becomes merely a poetic phrasing for a much larger problem. The place where it's crucial to have serious talks with my oldest two on how to respond to a simple police encounter, when I would never even think to have a conversation like that with my youngest two. How did we get to the place where people become so hardened and stubborn they refuse to even entertain the idea that maybe—just maybe—their ways of thinking need altering. God, how do I approach these people in love while at the same time confronting them of their need for change?

I saw the toddler faces of my boys morph into teenagers, their sweet innocence still lingering, but beginning to gain their own voice in this world. What would people see first? Jayden's heart and sensitivity to those around him, or his brown skin? Would people see Jaxon's sense of humor that could light up a whole room, or just another brown boy up to no good?

God, raise up these boys to be servant leaders for Your Kingdom! Let their voices be heard and not lost in the deafening noise of this shattered world. Protect them and go before them wherever they go. And God, build them up with Your love and Your kindness when people around them don't see and treasure them how You desire them to be treasured.

As I sat there, in that Sunday School class, I just couldn't believe that our world had come to this. I can understand how people have varying viewpoints about how our country should operate. I can respect differing opinions on how our country's money and resources should be used. What I *can't* wrap my head around is how eyes can look on a specific shade of brown and see anything other than just another *human being* made in the image of the Creator of this universe. How does *color* dictate worth? How does *color* represent deserved dignity? How does *color* define a *person? It doesn't!* So how come *color* is having to defend its every move?

I wondered what thoughts were going through Zach's mind as mine was racing in a million different directions. My husband is a very easy-going, roll with the punches kind of guy. I'm convinced he could answer any Bible question or NBA trivia given the opportunity, but he would *never* admit to it. His humility overshadows all he does and very few people truly know the depth of knowledge, love, and genuineness he possesses. He once taught himself Greek just to be able to find a new way to love the Word of God and has memorized *entire* books of the Bible. He's quiet in typical Sunday School settings and rarely volunteers an answer even though he would have the correct one 9.5 times out of 10 (I'm trying not to show partiality so you take me seriously) and usually leans over and whispers the correct answer in my ear. He wouldn't even be the first to volunteer to pray, simply because he never wants to draw attention to himself. These are characteristics that I both love and hate about my husband. I love his humility, but I hate that most people never get to see as much of him as I do and his deep, deep love for the Lord. It's a catch 22. When I look at my husband I see a picture of Jesus. Jesus knew all. He was *in* on the grand plan of the redemption story, but he wasn't boastful or arrogant in his knowledge. He was brought low to be made high. So when Zach raised his hand to respectfully counter another comment made in this specific Sunday School, and then volunteered to close out the class in prayer, I was convinced his heart was just as heavy as mine, even if I was the only one shedding the tears.

To my brothers and sisters of color, I want you to know I hear you. I have heard your unspoken (and sometimes spoken) very legitimate concerns of two white parents raising two young, black men. You are worried that they won't grow to truly love and appreciate their culture. You are worried that as a transracial adoptive family we will just *raise them white* along with their younger brothers. I promise you, we won't let you down. I promise to *continue* to show and teach our boys how to have pride in their heritage. I promise to *continue* to take them to the barber shop where they have been going since they were toddlers. I promise to *continue* to play gospel music and sing along to the songs so my boys see the love I have for the music created by their people. I promise to *continue* to live in a diverse neighborhood where they see and interact with people of all races and ethnicities. I promise to *continue* to humble myself and ask questions when I don't know the answer. I promise to *continue* to teach them about black history throughout the year and not just during the month of February. I promise to *continue* to love our boys with every fiber of my being until the day I die. I will fight for them, and I will make sure they have a voice in this world.

7

Final Call to the Church

I n my first book, I ended with a call to the church as a way to encourage believers to actively get involved in the mission of helping the most vulnerable population (James 1:27 —"Religion that is pure and undefiled before God the Father is this: to visit orphans and widows in their affliction, and to keep oneself unstained from the world"). As a final *call*, I feel burdened to leave you with one last message. This topic breeds debate and division, and for many it needs a revision.

I would say the vast majority of believers hold a pro-life stance (Psalm 139:13-14 —For you formed my inward parts; you knitted me together in my mother's womb. I praise you, for I am fearfully and wonderfully made. Wonderful are your works; my soul knows it very well). As image bearers of God, we believe *all* life, no matter the age, has great value because the Creator of the universe masterfully created that life.

However, somewhere along the way, people became so focused on pro-*birth* that they forgot their responsibility to defend the whole *life*. Do I believe pro-*birth* is important? Without a doubt! It is an essential part of my faith. Personally, I would find it impossible to defend the name of Christ while ignoring the unborn. So, the problem doesn't lie with being a person who defends the baby in the womb.

The problem lies with *stopping* at defending the baby in the womb. Far too many people put a *period* where there should be a *comma*, insinuating that the work is finished when the unborn are protected. To truly hold a pro-life stance, you must first have a heart for women in crisis situations. You must have a heart for people on the streets suffering with addictions they have tried unsuccessfully to break. Pro-life means being an advocate for family preservation and unification while understanding that adoption is actually a last resort, not merely a coveted solution to growing a family. Pro-life is an ongoing demonstration of choosing to love the ones who deem themselves unlovable, even at great cost to yourself.

Statistics show there are roughly ten million children worldwide living in institutions today. According to a 2019 study, "over 672,000 children spent time in U.S. foster care." One third of those children were people of color, and "more than 20,000 young people aged out of foster care without permanent families." Research has shown that those who leave care without being linked to forever families have a higher likelihood than youth in the general population to experience homelessness, unemployment, and incarceration as adults."[4] In 2019, approximately 630,000 legal abortions took place in the United Sates alone.[5] These numbers are impossible to grasp when you start trying to make sense that those thousands and millions are *faces*, not simply numbers on a page. Some would argue pro-life starts with the womb, but it can't possibly end there. And quite honestly, I would argue it starts well before the womb. In Matthew 25:35-40 Jesus gives an example of how to live out a countercultural love in response to those around us:

---

4. https://www.childrensrights.org/newsroom/fact-sheets/foster-care/

5. CDC Abortion Surveillance. "Number of legal abortions reported in the U.S. from 1973 to 2019."

"For I was hungry and you gave me food, I was thirsty and you gave me drink, I was a stranger and you welcomed me, I was naked and you clothed me, I was sick and you visited me, I was in prison and you came to me.' Then the righteous will answer him, saying, 'Lord, when did we see you hungry and feed you, or thirsty and give you drink? And when did we see you a stranger and welcome you, or naked and clothe you? And when did we see you sick or in prison and visit you?' And the King will answer them, 'Truly, I say to you, as you did it to one of the least of these my brothers, you did it to me.'"

Our world is desperate to know the hope found in Christ. Our world is desperately searching for a peace that goes beyond any human understanding. Our worst days are another person's dream day. We can't simply start and end our fight with the unborn; we have to fight for the *entire* vulnerable population. Our eyes need to search so much further than our bubble. Our hearts need to grow so much bigger than our comforts. Our arms need to stretch so much wider than our conveniences.

I have found, the times I am drawn closest to God are the times I am most stretched and inconvenienced by the *discomforts* of this world. When everything is smooth sailing, I have no reason to trust in anyone other than my fallible self. In my comforts, I am tempted to build up my *self*-worth with transient, earthly achievements and temporary successes. When the *discomforts* come, they pile up and weigh me down. It's in those moments I am forced to run to Christ. I am forced to step outside of *me*, and turn to the only One who can transform something broken into something beautiful. When my only choice is to run to Christ, I find time and time again that He is *all* I need. And though the discomforts often bring pain and heartache, God faithfully demonstrates His promise to never leave or forsake me. When I become inconvenienced to help others, God provides and blesses my endeavors. Those blessings sometimes come in the form of answered prayer exactly how I prayed and exactly how I wanted God to answer me. But those blessings have also come by way of trials I never wanted to face and heartache I never wanted to experience. Either way, my praise remains: "Worthy is the Lamb who was slain, to receive power and wealth and wisdom and might and honor and glory and blessing!" (Revelation 5:12).

As a mother of two children through adoption, you can imagine that I am a huge advocate for adoption. And you would be one hundred percent correct. But, since walking the adoption path with my boys and opening my ears to adult adoptee voices, I have also become a huge advocate for family preservation and unification. You can't have a heart for adoption without having a heart for the people who brought those children into the world. The love I have for our boys doesn't begin with them, but rather begins with who they came from.

I cringe when I hear people talk about adoption and the focus is *how long will it take to be matched, what are the chances of a disrupted match, how many matches does your agency make in a year.* And truth be told, I cringe because that used to be me! By God's grace that hasn't been me for a while, but there was a time when it definitely was me.

When adoption becomes more about *you* than about the child and his/her family, you aren't the right person for the job. Let me say that once more: If you are looking at adoption primarily to fill a gap in your life, you are *not* ready yet! Concerning adoption specifically, I want to challenge you today to expand your viewpoint. Refocus and really look at the whole picture. Become inconvenienced and uncomfortable to extend the love of Jesus. If you are new to adoption, or maybe you are seasoned but after reading this you are questioning your motives, go listen to the experts in this field. I'm not talking about the men and women who have racked up degrees learning about the field. I'm talking about the only ones who know more than any educational degree could ever provide: adoptees! Give them a platform and let them share their voice. Open your ears so they can open their hearts[6].

---

6. Practical ways to get involved: Become a licensed foster parent. Give financially, donate and/or volunteer at pregnancy centers (numerous opportunities to help serve in this specific area). Give financially or of your time to help mothers/fathers in crisis situations. Offer support to foster/ adoptive parents. Provide personal/family/church outreach opportunities to involve the local community and actively look for ways to fill specific needs.

8

Turn Their Eyes to Jesus

I had the textbook perfect response in a particular parenting situation back a few weeks ago. The way I handled myself and my specific child's sin was flawless and exactly the type of thing you would see in a best seller parenting book. I was dressed with the accessories of a gentle and quiet spirit and simultaneously high fiving my efforts. And guess what? Not a single thing I did worked! Let me try and paint you a picture.

I heard two of my boys bickering from the next room over as I prepared dinner in the kitchen. I remained calm and thought back to our latest Sunday School parenting class. The teacher for the class—let it also be noted that he owns his own counseling center and offers great real-life response for every situation—recounted a time his children were doing the same thing at a local pool. He had the two children hold hands and walk around the entire pool perimeter until they were laughing and had totally forgotten what they were originally fighting about in the first place. I thought, what better time than today to try out this wonderful method on my own children. I very sweetly called the boys inside without a single wrinkle of frustration on my face and told them to hold hands and walk around the entire downstairs until I could see a heart change. Confident that this would solve the problem in a matter of minutes I smiled as I walked back to the stove to give my taco meat another stir.

Well folks, I'm embarrassed to say after a few minutes passed, one child was still crying loud sobs of defeat, while the other child was beaming ear to ear. Wanting to avoid a potential dizzy spell from all the circling around the kitchen island, I proceeded to have them sit down together, still holding hands, on the floor beside me. Again, let me remind you, I *wore* confidence on my exterior and was so proud of my (failing) mothering decisions this particular evening. A few more minutes passed. The sobbing child was still exercising his resilience in bouts of tears and the beaming child was now speaking words of affirmation to his brother, "I love you more than ketchup!" And if you know this child, that's a *deep* love he's claiming, because the boy can seriously put away some ketchup. Since I had seen a successful heart change in "beaming child" I released him to the wild to go play. I sent "sobbing child" to a quiet room to calm down. After a few minutes I heard loud sobs of jumbled speech coming from my bedroom. I walked in, still wearing the robe of confidence, and asked, "Were you praying, baby?" to which he replied *yes*. Being the model mother in this particular parenting situation I proceeded, "Ya know what? Sometimes mommy cries out to God just like that. And what's so special about God is that He hears us and He is with us even when we are so sad and think no one else understands us. I know you feel so frustrated right now, and mommy really wants to help you. I'm on your side. I'm not trying to make you more mad. Can you tell me one thing mommy can do to help you calm down right now?" I mean, when I say I had all the right words, I had all.the.right.words! Do you think he stopped crying? Nope. Do you think I reached the point of throwing in the towel? Not a chance.

As we walked out, I started praying out loud on the couch where my boys could clearly hear me, partially in frustration but still trying to remain under control. I was growing weary, but I remembered Zach was working with the boys on Galatians 6:9 — "And let us not grow weary of doing good, for in due season we will reap, if we do not give up." I knew accepting failure wasn't in the cards tonight. I prayed for patience for myself and for a calm heart for my boy. And then I prayed, "God, I really feel like a Pharisee right now, but I'm not trying to be. Don't let my prayers just be empty and loud for no reason. I want my boys to *see* that when I don't know what to do, I run to You." I remained resilient.

This little boy may be winning the battle, but I will win this war!

I moved to the rocking chair and extended my arms to hold my boy who, at this point, was beyond exhausted both mentally and physically. I sat down and hugged him as I rocked him. I could sense his whole body starting to calm down as we embraced. His interrupted breathing had returned to normal. I hugged him close and prayed once again with him in my arms. Just when I thought we had moved past this dramatic ordeal, in walked "beaming child," still beaming, and it only took his little body being within ten feet of temporarily-calm "sobbing child" to send that one back into hysterics.

The evening continued about like the last couple paragraphs with highs and lows and ups and downs until an early bedtime was had by all. I say all this to say that perfect parenting simply isn't reality no matter how picture perfect a family portrays itself on the outside. You can parent by the book and still not get the right results. So although failure tries to claim a seat at your side, let me encourage you that God's peace is sufficient for the day. And when you lose all control, He remains on His throne, still Holy, still omniscient, still full of grace and mercy.

The honest truth is motherhood doesn't always look *happy*. Many days I feel like I'm hanging by a thread, trying to keep my head afloat, and four little boys safe from their own created chaos. BUT, I want my message to be that though I may be weak, in my weakness my Father is made strong. 2 Corinthians 12:9 says, "But he said to me, 'My grace is sufficient for you, for my power is made perfect in weakness.' Therefore I will boast all the more gladly of my weaknesses, so that the power of Christ may rest upon me." I may be weary, but I have a Father who has called me to lay my burdens at His feet (Matthew 11:28 — "Come to me, all who labor and are heavy laden, and I will give you rest").

I don't want to be stuck in the *tired* and the *unhappy*. I don't want to dwell in the *hard*. I want to acknowledge the *difficult*, and run to the One who can fill my cup.

As a mom of four very busy boys five and under, I have learned that pointing my kids to Jesus doesn't always look like a nice row of perfectly placed toddlers sitting quiet as a churchmouse at the dining room table for family devotions. Does it look like that sometimes? Sure, but when we make it part of the everyday, we have seen that our boys begin to have *hearts* to learn more about God's Word, rather than something just done out of vain repetition. And hearts for God is what I desire for my boys.

I want my kids to know Jesus. I want them to develop a love for Jesus at an early age. I want to soak their minds with deep rooted truths while they are young so when they grow they can rely on those same truths to help guide them in their endeavors. I've learned that making them sit still and silent just isn't the way those truths are going to be ingrained and imprinted on their hearts. Now, are there times to learn the importance of a still and quiet spirit? Yes, absolutely! But I have learned that the truths tend to stick better when they are learned through the mundane, daily moments of simply living life in light of the gospel.

From one weary and tired momma to another, we're all just looking for opportunities to point our babies to Jesus, build their character, and manage the chaos. Here is a list of practical ways we've worked toward this goal in our home. Please find links and information for many of these items in the "Resources" section at the end of the book.

- **Evening Family Devotions** — We've tried this a myriad of different ways. Zach is an extremely fast eater, and he beats us all at dinnertime. So our most recent attempt has been Zach reading through a few chapters of the Bible after he finishes eating but while the rest of us are all still gathered around the dinner table.

- **Catechism** — *New City Catechism* has an app you can download on your phone that goes through 52 questions. If you switch to the kids version they have a song that corresponds to each question/answer to help with memorization. The songs are simple, but catchy and my boys love listening to them.

- **Daily Audio Bible (Kids Channel)** — This is a short, roughly five to ten minute podcast. We are currently going through the New Testament in a year, and in this podcast specifically, a child reads the Bible passage with his parents. They do a quick recap and close in prayer. It's not anything too deep, but we are using it as a way to teach the importance of daily devotions. And my boys enjoy listening to the Bible being read by a young child.

- **Praying for accidents** — This is something I've tried to be very consistent with as we drive on the road. When the boys were young, whenever we would pass by an accident I would pray out loud so they heard me. I made a point to pray for the people involved in the accident and also thanked God for the first responders. Now that they are older, I can see they have picked this up and often, even when I miss the accident, one will yell out, "Mommy! Accident! We need to pray!" Accidents have also been a great way to teach patience. We travel a very high traffic interstate. Often, because of the times we travel we aren't affected, but certain times of day, you can count on heavy traffic. And if there is an accident or there is any amount of rain (I'm convinced southerners can't drive in the rain) the traffic only worsens. In these times, it's very easy to get impatient and frustrated. But I've learned that when I display those emotions they are quickly mimicked by my kiddos. So I have tried to use "heavy traffic" as a way to thank God for our safety. I try to teach the kids that maybe God is sparing us from being in a terrible accident where we would have otherwise gotten hurt or injured. It's also been a great way to sneak in a few early driver education lessons. Personally, I get annoyed when other drivers feel entitled to break the law because their destination is somehow more important than mine. So when other cars decide to use the strip of road to the right of the far right lane and fly past everyone else in traffic to skip ahead to their exit, my boys and I have started to yell, "LAWBREAKERS! STOP BREAKING THE LAW!" And I think it accidentally turned into a game of who can yell the loudest. When we see people texting in the vehicle beside us, we do the same thing. We've been able to talk about different distractions that cause people to have accidents. Honestly, I feel very good about the extra driving education they are receiving at age five and three and hope I can somehow convince our insurance company to knock off a few bucks when I have four teenage male drivers in the house in a few years.

- **Bible for Kids App** — I give so much credit to this app for teaching my boys Bible stories. There was a time, and still oftentimes it is true, that they would choose this app over any app on the iPad. The app is an interactive way for children to explore the stories of the Bible hands-on. My boys have memorized full stories from this app simply because they never tire of listening to them more than once.

- **Praying on the way to school** — As we drive to school each morning I try to be intentional about each of us praying for our day. At first, the boys' prayers were very self-focused. I tried to encourage them to think of one another as they prayed. And now, not always, but most of their prayers are for each other. Jaxon prays for Jayden to have a good day at school and Jayden prays for his brothers to have a good day playing at home with mommy. It's a simple but intentional way to teach selflessness.

- **Prayers for your kids** — Bob Hostetler created "31 Biblical Virtues to pray for your kids." It's a small bookmark size sheet that has different virtues listed with a corresponding verse. It's a great tool I have kept on my bathroom mirror as a reminder to pray specifically for my children. And since there are 31 virtues, it's easy to take one a day and pray through the month.

- **Scripture Songs** — In 1990, Steve Green released *Hide 'Em In Your Heart: Bible Memory Melodies*. While this album is decades old, the songs are still so applicable and fun for the kids to enjoy. Shai Linne has a hip-hop album titled *Jesus Kids* that is also a great resource. He takes foundational truths and puts them to music. From one of the songs on the album, he published a children's book titled: *God Made Me and You: Celebrating God's Design for Ethnic Diversity*. I would highly recommend it. *The Ology* by *Sovereign Grace* is another great one along the same lines incorporating deep biblical truths for children to learn. I used to play a mix of all these songs in the background as the boys played downstairs or while we ate lunch. The songs are great scriptures put to music, sung by children. I specifically remember one day not playing it, and my boys were walking in and out of the kitchen just singing one of the songs quietly. Until then, I didn't even realize they had the songs memorized.

- **Toddler Chores** — I wasn't one of those kids who grew up with chores. I think my mom was definitely on the losing end with this particular parenting choice back in the '90s. When I first became a mom, other mom friends would tell me stories of their two and three year olds helping out with chores around the house. I'd smile and have the *my children weren't born in the 1800s and this isn't Little House on the Prairie* conversation inside my own head. But let me tell you something, two and three year olds *can* do chores. In fact, they are so naive that they actually think doing chores is, dare I say, *fun!* Yes, moms! There is a small subset of crazy people in this world, whom we refer to as toddlers, who are perfect for the job. I would not recommend paying by the hour, since they tend to drag out a five minute task to about 10-15 minutes, and they definitely don't get the job completed the same way you would as they have a much different approach, *but* you wont regret starting chores with toddlers. The first chore I usually implement is unloading the dishwasher. I teach them what dishes go on the drying rack, they learn to sort big and small utensils in the right drawer organizers, and I only ever put sharp knives in one section of the utensil dishwasher tray and they learn those are only for mommy to touch. I've taught my boys to recognize when our dog needs to go outside and to let her back in when she's waiting patiently at the door. I have a small handheld vacuum that they fight over to clean up crumbs from snack time. We have a mop that squirts out a spay and they have learned how many sprays to squirt while cleaning the floors (another job they *ask* me if they can do) and they put their own laundry away in their drawers. They are capable of so much more than we think and they, for the most part, really love to help!

- **The Man Card** — One of my favorites! And one of my "mom-wins" that Zach credits as genius! I don't have many of those, so I'm really reveling in this one. I realize I'm 100% biased, but I have some pretty great boys. They are sweet, thoughtful, loving, funny, the list could go on and on. But one thing my boys are is SHY! People often come up to them at church, in school, or out in public and speak to them. If you're lucky, you may get a small smirk before they try to bury their head in my leg. Or, if they do manage to utter a response, it's about as quiet as a needle dropping into a haystack. So, on a stroke of genius and stupid intermingled, I invented the MAN CARD! I grabbed some credit card sized cardstock and wrote MAN CARD on about ten pieces. I told them every time I saw them stepping out of their comfort zone to be kind or respectful I would give them a card! Y'all, that's All. I. Did! And you would have thought I was handing out hundred dollar bills for the taking. At first, I would coach them on the way to church: "Ok, if Pastor comes up and says, 'Good morning' to you, you shake his hand, look him in the eyes, and say, 'Good morning' back." Then the bar was raised. "Hey! Who wants to earn THREE man cards?! If you go up to someone and say hello to them before they say hello to you, I'll give you THREE, not just one."

- **Put off/ Put on notebook** — When our kids disobey, we try to prioritize sitting down with them and talking about what they did and why it was wrong. As they've gotten older, we've used their acts of disobedience as a way to teach repentance and the importance of going to God in prayer. We've implemented a "put off/put on" notebook as a tool we use from time to time. They sit in a designated time-out section of our house and complete the notebook page. Since they are still too young to write full sentences, I have them draw a picture in the "put off" column of what they did wrong. In the "put on" column, they draw a picture of what they should have done instead. As they grow, the third column will be used to write either one word or one verse that goes along with the correct choice they should have made. Once they have completed the drawings, there is a small box for them to check once they have prayed alone and asked God for forgiveness and for help to make the right choices before either Zach or I go in to follow up.

- **10 commandments hand motions** — When I first taught the 10 Commandments to our boys I used the song from the *New City Catechism* (mentioned above). I also found this video to be helpful to teach the motions along with the song: "Teaching Kids the 10 Commandments!" I like how each motion uses the number of fingers to correspond to the number commandment being talked about. I used this when they were very young and haven't re-taught it in a while and they still have all the motions memorized. It's a simple but great way to teach the 10 commandments.

- **Scripture memory** — You would be surprised how much young toddlers can memorize. I specifically remember working on scripture memory with Jayden, not paying too much attention to Jaxon (assuming he was too young to really understand). And one morning while I was quizzing Jayden, Jaxon walked up to us and recited the entire verse. I was floored. Another time, Jordy wasn't yet two years old and he was sitting in on our church's VBS. On the final night, out of the blue, he started reciting phrases from the memory verse the boys and girls were learning that week and doing the hand motions to the songs right along with the big kids. Never again will I underestimate what a young child can learn given the opportunity.

- **Meaning of song lyrics** — I remember, as a little girl, listening to songs either on the radio or cassettes and my dad pausing to have my brother or I tell him what the lyrics meant from time to time. Being the minister of music at our church and coming from a very musical family, it was probably ingrained in him and he must have passed that trait down to me. I enjoy listening to the intricacy of lyrics just as much as a good melody. The other day, the boys and I were listening to a gospel song while driving in the car, and part of the lyrics said, "He will fix it." I turned down the volume and used those lyrics as an opportunity to teach the boys that God, without a doubt, will *fix* our problems, but the way he *fixes* them won't always be the way we prayed for them to be fixed. I further explained that God will bless us in ways where He can be most glorified in and through our lives.

- **Resurrection Easter eggs** — I've seen many, slightly different versions of this idea, but essentially there are twelve plastic eggs filled with tiny figurine items related to the resurrection story. We started this when Jayden was around two or three years old and did one egg a night leading up to Easter. Both boys have really enjoyed this tradition and it has helped them understand the resurrection story on a deeper level. They beg to open a new egg each day and there's no chance of us skipping a night because they won't let us forget.

- **Jesus Storybook Bible** —There are plenty of wonderful Children's Bibles, but we love this specific one. Each Bible story focuses the attention back on the ultimate story of God's grand rescue plan: to send His Son, Jesus, to die on the cross and take the sins of mankind (Romans 5:8 — "...but God shows his love for us in that while we were still sinners, Christ died for us").

- **Asking your kids to pray for you** — God has used this one to humble me on many occasions. One day in particular I remember the boys having a really hard day arguing with each other. I felt as though every five minutes I was addressing one or more of them for not treating each other kindly. Out of the blue, while I was preparing lunch, Jayden asked if he could pray. *Wonderful! Maybe he's finally listening to what I have been saying all day. He desperately needs a heart change, so I'm glad he wants to pray for that.* I closed my eyes as he prayed, and much to my surprise, instead of praying for *his* attitude to change, he prayed that *mine* would. Nothing humbles you more than your child praying for your attitude. And as he was praying, I realized I had become so frustrated with their disobedience, I failed to respond correctly in demonstrating a heart of Jesus myself.

- **1,2,3** — A piece of advice someone shared with me as a new mother was to never use the "I'm going to count to three..." as an incentive for a child to obey. I grew up with this technique, like most kids, but at the root of that statement is an allowance for your *child* to dictate when he/she chooses to obey you or not. You're giving your child permission to ignore quick obedience. Since our boys were young, we have used the phrase, "Obey right away, all the way, with a happy heart." If you were to ask my children, "How do you obey?" I am confident they would spout out that phrase because they have heard it so many times.

As parents we are going to have moments of victory, but we are also going to experience a lot of failure. Consistency in the things that truly matter is *key*. Pointing our babies to Jesus is *key*. Raising our children to love the Lord their God with all their heart, soul, and mind and loving others as they would love themselves is the greatest commandment Jesus gives (Matthew 22:26-40). In order to remain consistent in the things that truly matter, we must have grace and mercy new every day. Lamentations 3:22-23 says, "The steadfast love of the Lord never ceases; his mercies never come to an end; they are new every morning; great is your faithfulness." God shows His great mercy to us, His children, day after day, moment after moment. In light of such great mercy we have received, we ought to emulate our Father in extending mercy to our children.

9
Reaping in Joy

I hate the title of this chapter.

I guess to tell you why I hate it, I should first tell you why I love it. I love that it allows the theme verse (Psalm 126:5—Those who sow in tears shall reap with shouts of joy) to come full circle. First, I metaphorically sowed in tears and then I reaped with joy. The title allows the reader to see where my path to motherhood began. For that reason, I love the title. And obviously my love for it outweighed the hate.

But I hate it because I don't want people to read the title in ignorance. I don't want people to assume, *Oh, she was really sad at first and she only became joyful when she finally got pregnant.* That statement couldn't be further from the truth. I can look back at my infertility with great joy. An unexplainable joy, actually. A joy I never wanted and would never wish on anyone, but a joy I can't imagine my life without. My pregnancies, while they brought great happiness, never for a second outweighed the joy in bringing our oldest two home from the hospital. And before you go saying, *Well, that sounds nice, but she is basically obligated to say that,* that mentality is the very reason I hate my title. *Adoption* is actually where the reaping of joy began and it only continued with the same level of enthusiasm with each added boy. I was only able to reap with joy because of the tears that I had sown.

In life you will, without a doubt, face many times of sowing in tears. A loved one will pass unexpectedly, families will be torn apart, hopes and dreams will be shattered. It's inevitable. I would say looking back on the last three decades, I've lived a *good life*. But it's been a life of sowing in tears.

As a young child I remember sitting in the chairs of the funeral home saying goodbye to great grandparents knowing family reunions would never be the same.

Sowing in tears.

As a teenager, I saw my parents' marriage fall apart in front of my eyes and tried with everything in me to change the trajectory with no success. Memories and traditions ended abruptly, and I never got to savor the *one last time.*

Sowing in tears.

As an adult I watched dreams fade into the distance with no chance of survival. I saw motherhood dangling in front of me, just out of reach, more times than I can count.

Sowing in tears.

BUT, *May the God of hope fill you with all joy and peace in believing, so that by the power of the Holy Spirit you may abound in hope* (Romans 15:13). I never once sowed alone. I wept, but not a single tear was wasted. God saw every single one. Can you even imagine that? Of all the billions of people living on this planet, God saw *every* tear that fell from *my* eyes. In fact, He knew of my sorrow before I even knew myself, and He was preparing me for my very trials long before I ever knew they would exist. When I was walking my most lonely days,

He stood by my side. When I would go to my room and cry in secret, He held me in the palm of His hand. When I saw no light ahead, He guided my path. He is sovereign in the big and He is sovereign in the small. And as I sowed, I also reaped.

As a young child I grew up in a home with two wonderful parents who taught me, by example, to love the Lord. I grew up with both sets of grandparents a stone's throw away where I can look back with fondest memories of time spent with them.

Reaping in joy.

As a teenager, I saw an example of my Heavenly Father through my earthly one. I would often find my dad up early in the morning and up late at night, sitting in his recliner with a journal on one knee and his torn and tattered Bible on his other knee. I saw a broken man glued together by his unwavering faith in the Father.

Reaping in joy.

As an adult, I saw another example of my Heavenly Father in the man who would become my husband. Another man who was up early each morning rooting himself deep in God's word.

Reaping in joy.

John Piper once said, "I've never heard anyone say the really deep lessons of life have come in times of ease and comfort. But, I have heard many saints say every significant advance I've ever made in grasping in the depth of God's love and growing deep with Him, have come through suffering." This one statement sums up the very essence of my story. I want God to be glorified and on display through my suffering. When we suffer well, our suffering doesn't have to be wasted. Our tears can have purpose. Our pain can sprout beauty. God, on His throne, can be glorified.

The message of my testimony has been how God worked through my affliction and brought praise. I have shared the story of how He transformed brokenness to beauty, infertility to fertility, sorrow to joy, and how His strength was showcased in my weakness. All of those are powerful messages in and of themselves. But the message I want to leave you, my readers, with is the most important message of all. This message has the power to transform your life from the inside out. It's the message of redemption— "...Christ Jesus, who, though he was in the form of God, did not count equality with God a thing to be grasped, but emptied himself, by taking the form of a servant, being born in the likeness of men. And being found in human form, he humbled himself by becoming obedient to the point of death, even death on a cross (Philippians 2:5-8)."

I've memorized this verse several times in my life, as a little girl in Sunday School and even as an adult. But it took me until writing this chapter in my book to truly grasp the weight these words carry. Jesus Christ is One with His Father. The Father, Son, and Holy Spirit are three persons in *one* God. Each one plays a different role, but at the core, they are *one!* So when this verse speaks of Christ holding the *form of God* but instead *emptying* Himself and *humbling* Himself in obedience to His Father to die on the cross for *me*, I stand amazed and overwhelmed.

We all entered this world as sinners, in direct rebellion against God (Romans 3:23 "For all have sinned and fall short of the glory of God). And as Paul reminds us, even when we desperately *want* to do good, we still fall short time and time again because of our sin nature in a sin-cursed world (Romans 7:18-20: "For I know that nothing good dwells in me, that is, in my flesh. For I have the desire to do what is right, but not the ability to carry it out. For I do not do the good I want, but the evil I do not want is what I keep on doing. Now if I do what I do not want, it is no longer I who do it, but sin that dwells within me"). When we come to the realization that God *sees* our sin, He loves us *in spite* of our sin, and He *carried* our sin on the cross and *saved* us from the very sin that nailed Him there, how can we not stand in awe? Who am I that He would love me so? Who am I that He would show me such great mercy?

Before His death on the cross, Jesus held the most impactful ministry of all time as He visited surrounding towns to spread the news of the Gospel. One of the messages He gave was the parable of the four soils. He spoke to reveal the mysteries of the Kingdom of God to a vast group of people. Mark 4:1-9:

> "Again he began to teach beside the sea. And a very large crowd gathered about him, so that he got into a boat and sat in it on the sea, and the whole crowd was beside the sea on the land. And he was teaching them many things in parables, and in his teaching he said to them: "Listen! Behold, a sower went out to sow. And as he sowed, some seed fell along the path, and the birds came and devoured it. Other seed fell on rocky ground, where it did not have much soil, and immediately it sprang up, since it had no depth of soil. And when the sun rose, it was scorched, and since it had no root, it withered away. Other seed fell among thorns, and the thorns grew up and choked it, and it yielded no grain. And other seeds fell into good soil and produced grain, growing up and increasing and yielding thirtyfold and sixtyfold and a hundredfold." And he said, "He who has ears to hear, let him hear."

Later in the passage, Jesus interprets this message to His disciples. The seed sown on the path represents the hardened hearts. Satan is active almost immediately with this scenario and eyes are blinded to the truth of the Gospel. The seed sown on the rocky ground represents those who receive the Gospel with only a temporary joy. These are the ones who immediately fall away when afflictions come. The seed sown among the thorns represents the ones who hear the Word and know the Word, but let the worries of the world take hold of them rather than the peace found in Christ. Their desires for the riches of the world captivate their attention rather than true satisfaction in Christ. The seed sown on the good soil, though, represents the chosen ones who not only *hear* and *accept* the Word of God, but also *bear fruit* because of it. The sowing of the Gospel message is a picture of God's sovereignty. God's love is a reaching love. His love actively finds you where you are, even if where you are feels unworthy of any love, let alone a love from a Holy God. To those He chose before the foundations of the world, He reaches down and carries you to a seat at His table, a place He has prepared just for *you*.

My prayer for you is that you would have ears to hear and eyes to see the gift that is salvation in Christ alone. I pray you would prepare your heart so that the seed, that is the Word of God, planted in your life doesn't fall on the path or the rocky or thorny ground, but that it falls on *good soil!* Salvation is more than a pinpointed date pointing to a single prayer you prayed one time in your life. True salvation in Christ is faith and repentance resulting in Kingdom-first living. True salvation in Christ is demonstrated by spiritual growth and lasting fruit. If you can pinpoint a time in your life where you prayed a prayer of salvation, but you're living a life contrary to that prayer, I would encourage you to search your heart. Your eternal destination is far more important than a chance of Russian roulette. If everything I'm saying turns out in the end to be a big sham, then nothing really changes. No harm, no foul. But, in the end, if what I'm saying is true, if there really is a God who sent His Son to die on the cross and be raised to life so you could be saved from eternal damnation, then *everything* I'm saying matters. I don't want to come to the end of my days and wonder how I will spend eternity. I want to *know* and have *confidence* that when my time on earth is through, I will be greeted by my Heavenly Father in all His majesty and hear Him say, "Well done, my child. Welcome home!"

Friend, whatever you are facing right now, whatever trial has you sowing in tears, run to Christ. God has not turned His back on you. He hasn't placed you to the side to focus His attention on someone more "put together." He sees you exactly where you are, in all your filth, in all your pain, and in all your rags. But He doesn't see the filth. He sees beauty. He doesn't see the pain. He sees redemption's blood shed on the cross. He doesn't see the rags. He sees Christ's *finished* work on the cross for those who believe in His saving grace. You can come as you are with the confidence that God is already at work turning your brokenness into beauty.

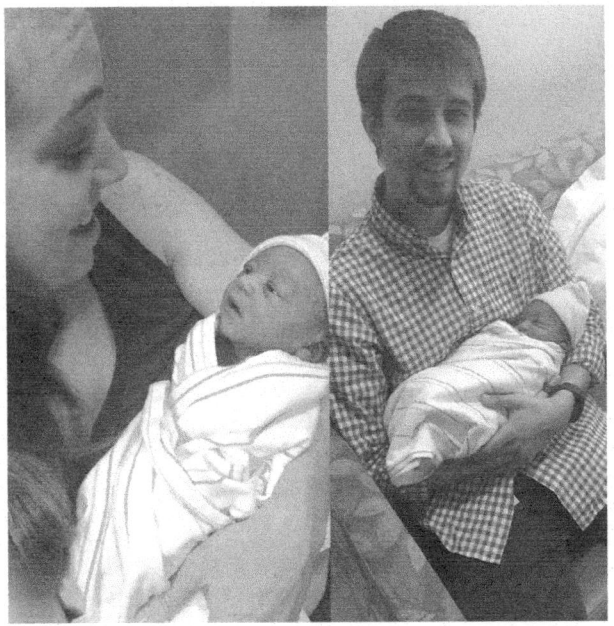

Holding Jaxon for the first time in our hospital room (August 2018).

One of the first pictures as a family of four (September 2018)
and family vacation almost one year later (July 2019).

Our family of four (October/November 2019).

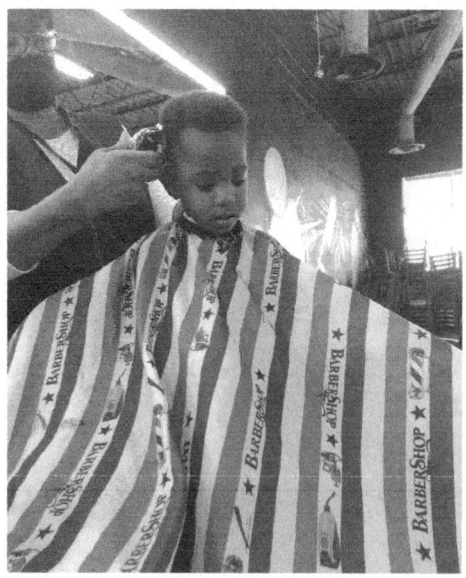

Jayden's first trip to the barber shop with Ms. Tina (June 2020).

Pregnant with Jordan. Last picture with our family of four (August 2020).

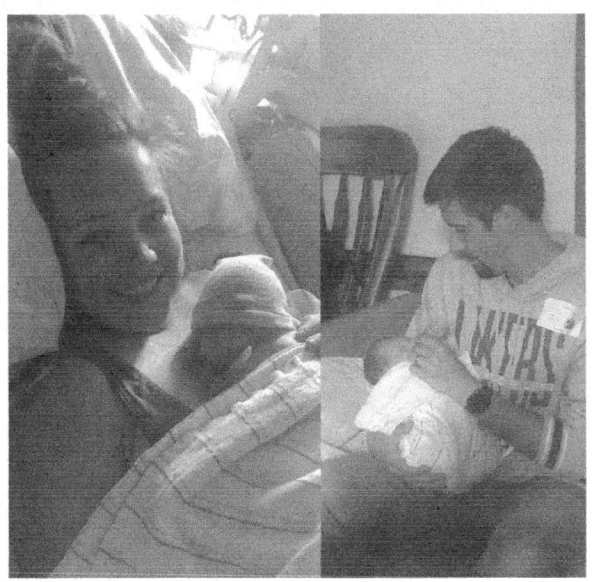

Jordan is born (August 2020).

One of the first pictures as a family of five (August 2020).
Three little Lakers fans (September/ November 2020).

Trip to Maine in the winter (Jayden—4 years old, Jaxon—
2 years old, Jordy—6 months old (February 2021).

First days with baby Jordy/ Mother's Day (August 2020/ May 2021).

Family vacation (June 2021).

Pregnant with Joshua (May 2021/ June 2021/ November 2021).

Trip to Iceland and 5 months pregnant with Joshua (August 2021).

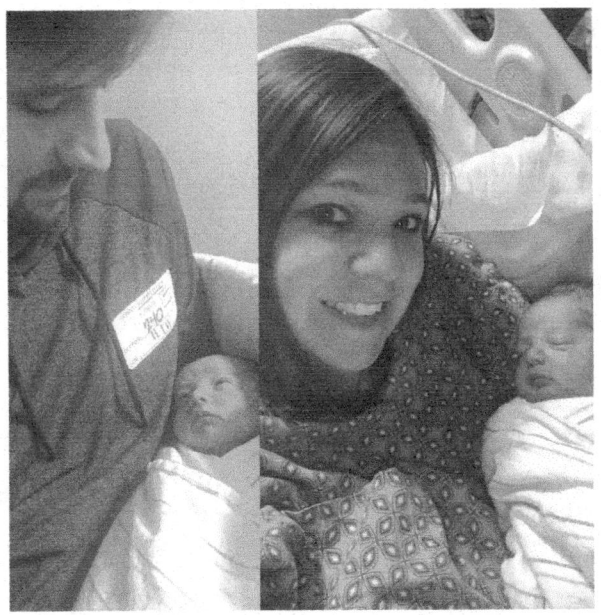

Joshua arrives with 29 minutes to spare to share a birthday
with big brother Jayden (November 2021).

Big brothers meet Joshua for the first time (November 2021).

Thanksgiving and Christmas (2021).

Family of six. Jayden—5 years old, Jaxon—3 years old, Jordy—
1 year old, Joshua—3 months old (February 2022).

They may outgrow the rocking chair, but they will never outgrow my arms. (December 2021/ May 2022/ July 2022).

We finally got to Israel. En Gedi, Jordan River (Jordan's namesake), Shilo (reading Hannah's prayer in 1 Samuel 2:1-10 in likely the same vicinity she would have prayed earnestly for a child), Sea of Galilee (August 2022).

If you think our hands are full, you should see our hearts
(June 2022/ July 2022/ September 2022).

Resources and Citations

Books

Hudson, Wade. *Pass It On: African American Poetry for Children.* Illustrated by Floyd Cooper, Scholastic Press, March 1993.

Linne, Shai. *God Made Me and You: Celebrating God's Design for Ethnic Diversity.* Illustrated by Trish Mahoney, New Growth Press, September 2018.

Lloyd-Jones, Sally. *The Jesus Storybook Bible,* ZonderKidz, 2007.

Music

Herms, Bernie, Hillary Scott, and Emily Weisband. "Thy Will," *Love Remains,* EMI Nashville, 2016.

Green, Steve. *Hide 'em in your heart vol. 1,* Sparrow Records, 2005.

Linne, Shai. *Jesus Kids.* SDGFella Music, 21 September 2018.

The Ology: Ancient Truths Ever New. Produced by Ben Gowell. Sovereign Grace Kids, October 2015.

Adoption and Abortion statistics

U.S. Department of Health and Human Services, Administration for Children and Families, Administration on Children, Youth and Families, Children's Bureau, https://www.acf.hhs.gov/cb. https://www.acf.hhs.gov/sites/default/files/documents/cb/afcarsreport27.pdf

Courtney, M., Dworsky, A., Brown, A., Cary, C., Love, K., & Vorhies, V. (2011). Midwest evaluation of the adult functioning of former foster youth: Outcomes at age 26. Chicago, IL: Chapin Hall at the University of Chicago. https://www. chapinhall.org/wp-content/uploads/Midwest-Eval-Outcomes-at-Age-26.pdf.

CDC Abortion Surveillance. "Number of legal abortions reported in the U.S. from 1973 to 2019." https://www.statista. com/statistics/185274/number-of-legal-abortions-in-the-us-since-2000/

Overview of Foster Care, Adoption, and other issues related to child welfare from ChildrensRights.org. https:// www.childrensrights.org/newsroom/fact-sheets/foster-care/#:~:text=On%20any%20given%20day%2C%20there,for%20 five%20or%20more%20years.

Smartphone Apps and Other Media

New City Catechism, The Gospel Coalition and Redeemer Presbyterian Church, © 2017. http://newcitycatechism.com/

Daily Audio Bible. https://dailyaudiobible.com/resources/mobile-app/

Bible App for Kids. Created by Life.Church https://apps.apple.com/ us/app/bible-app-for-kids/id668692393

"Teaching Kids the 10 Commandments!" YouTube.com. *Called to Cultivate,* 19 September 2016. https://youtu.be/auBp1tiiD7c

31 Ways to Pray for Your Kids App. Created by Bob Hostetler. http:// www.bobhostetler.com/31-ways-to-pray-app

Organizations

Lowcountry Biblical Counseling Center. http://www.lcbcc.org

Activities

Resurrection Easter eggs https://www.amazon.com/Family-Life-Resurrection-Eggs-Religious/dp/1602006512/ref=asc_df_1602006512/?tag=hyprod-20&linkCode=df0&hvadid=312031083993&hvpos=&hvnetw=g&hvrand=16041735642840000575&hvpone=&hvptwo=&hvqmt=&hvdev=c&hvdvcmdl=&hvlocint=&hvlocphy=9077370&hvtargid=pla-570263982170&psc=1

Guest Appearances

Infant Adoption Guide Podcast - Episode 93

https://infantadoptionguide.com/sowing-in-tears-a-mothers-sorrow-in-infertility-and-joy-in-adoption-with-leeann-hale-podcast-episode-93/

What the Fertility Podcast - Episode 18

https://www.whatthefertilitypod.com/podcast-episodes/episode18-infertilityandadoption-withleeannhale

Speaking Engagements

https://www.youtube.com/channel/UCWBrntRH4IevX8DN_cI66dQ

Connect with Me

Email—sowingintearsbook@gmail.com

Facebook—https://www.facebook.com/sowingintearsbook

Instagram—@sowingintearsbook